# HOW TO GLOW UP AS YOU GROW UP

## Your Go-To Guide for Overcoming Obstacles and Making Lemonade

by
**TERRI LOMAX**

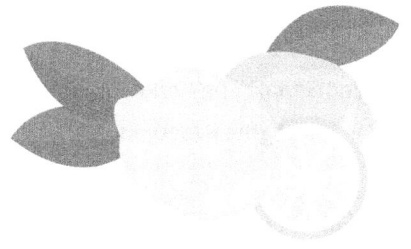

# cooLbooks

How To Glow Up As You Grow Up:
Your Go-To Guide for Overcoming Obstacles and Making Lemonade.
by Terri Lomax

Copyright @ 2020 CoolSpeak. The Youth Engagement Company
All Rights Reserved

Portrait photography by Krista Marie Photography
Cover & Layout Design by Iske Conradie
Proofreading by Sarina Cornthwaite

ISBN: 978-0-578-73290-9

# DEDICATION

To Jeannette Delores Lomax, my late maternal grandmother, whom I affectionately called, "Mommom." Thank you for being the Matriarch of the family. Thank you for believing in me, instilling a selfless spirit in me, and giving our family the opportunity to stand on your shoulders and go farther than previous generations have gone. You will always live in my heart, and I will make sure your legacy lives on through me and my work. I'm so sad you moved to the other side in the midst of my book being published, but I know you're here in spirit.

Your grandbaby,

Terri (or as you affectionately called me, "Shug")

# CONTENTS

## INTRODUCTION

**A Glimpse Into My Past**
8-9

**Why You Should Read This Book**
10-11

**Chapter 1: Start Here**
12-19

# THE JUICE

**Chapter 2: The Big Pitcher**
20-26

**Chapter 3: The Main Squeeze**
27 - 59

**Chapter 4: The Sugar F.A.C.E**
60 - 95

**Chapter 5: Just Stir and Add Water**
96 - 113

**Chapter 6: Make Lemonade and Share it**
114 - 125

# Glimpse Into My Past

**Before we get into introductions, I want to share my story with you. If we were to take a step back and view my life from a bird's eye-view, the timeline below pinpoints some of the most pivotal moments in my life.**

In the following pages, I'm going to show you how a little black girl from Philadelphia defied statistics about children with incarcerated parents, and made her dreams come true in the midst of some of the most traumatic experiences. This isn't just another self-help book, I'm giving you the cheat codes that you can use to glow up as you grow up (or evolve), and make your dreams come true too.

Despite all the obstacles I've faced, I've learned so many valuable lessons that I hope I can share with you in order to make your journey a bit smoother. You can look forward to real life stories, intimate details about my struggles, and activities to empower you to tackle your own obstacles through guided worksheets. I'll see you on the other side!

**NOVEMBER 23RD -** Born

**INFANCY -** Almost died from Meningitis.

**AGE 1 -** Met my amazing father for the first time.

**AGE 4 -** Molested.

**AGE 6 -** Felt God.

**AGE 7 -** The first time I remember visiting my mom in prison.

**AGE 8 -** Became a big sister (twice in one year).

**AGE 9 -** My entrepreneurial spirit was birthed. My sister and I asked my mom if we could go door to door to clean people's houses for money.

**AGE 11 -** Relocated from San Diego to Philadelphia.

**AGES 12-16 -** Silently suffered from depression, anxiety, and low self-esteem.

**AGE 17 -** Lost one of the most prominent male figures in my life, one month before I went away to college. I called him Daddy.

**AGE 18 -** Almost committed suicide because I felt the weight of the world on my shoulders. My siblings saved me.

**AGE 19 -** Had my first real relationship.

**AGE 21 -** Gave my first big speech in front of thousands during my Commencement ceremony at Kutztown University.

**AGE 22 -** Created the Mocha Girls Pit Stop blog because I had dreams of being an author, but was too scared to write a book.

**AGE 23 -** Earned my Master's degree in Conflict Analysis and Dispute Resolution from Salisbury University, and moved to NYC for my first big girl job.

**AGE 25 -** Married one of the greatest men I know.

**AGE 26 -** Worked for Facebook and two other Bay Area companies.

**AGE 27 -** Hired two team members to help me run my blog and found my biological father on Ancestry.com.

**AGE 28 -** Spoke at one of my first big tech conferences.

**AGE 29 -** I wrote this book for you... and I'm just getting started.

# Why you should read this book

Here's the thing- I'm not here to tell you how to live your life and I'm not here to preach to you. I wrote this book because quite frankly, my life sucked for a long time but I know I have something to offer. I've been through so much and although life has given me so many lemons... I'm still here.

During some of my darkest moments, I used to pray and tell God that if he would allow me to make it through to the other side, I would share my story and help others overcome their obstacles.

## "I'm not your mama or your teacher, I'm more like a sister friend."

I've gained a lot of wisdom because of all of the experiences I've lived through, and I can now share some shortcuts that you might be able to use.

You know how it is... we have our parents, elders, or other adults in our lives telling us stuff, and we either don't believe them, or we want to do what we want to do and see things for ourselves. I get that.

The thing is, I've learned that we don't always need to have a certain experience to learn from it. We can also learn from the mistakes and successes of others. Growing up, I witnessed many behaviors and lifestyles that seemed fun and lit at the time, but I had a feeling that they wouldn't be good for me in the future.

For example, I saw a lot of kids my age doing drugs, selling drugs, stealing, and making decisions that could negatively impact their lives. Now this is a judgement-free zone, but at the same time, we have to be honest about how our actions today impact the future tomorrow.

I'm not your mama or your teacher, I'm more like your sister friend. I'm going to share tips, resources, and advice that could change your life for the better, if you choose to use them.

**All the stories in this book are true stories based on what I remember from my life. I really hope that you can use these activities and lessons to enhance your life and go farther than I have!**

I'm a living witness that we are not defined by where we come from, what we come from, or what happened to us. We have the power to choose how far we go. Period!

# Chapter 1
# Start here

**My name is Terri Lomax and according to statistics, I should have been an alcoholic. I should have been a high school dropout, a teen mom, a prison inmate, or living below the poverty line.**

According to statistics, I shouldn't be here today, but I am.

Based on where I come from, what I look like and what has happened to me, society says I should be a lot of different things; many of them aren't desirable or good.

Although I may not know you personally, chances are if you're reading this, you might have some of those same statistics stacked against you.

Here's the thing though: I kind of like proving people wrong. I get a kick out of doing what's said to be impossible, and I honestly don't like people telling me what I can't do.

I was raised in an abusive household where I was verbally and physically abused. My mom had also been in and out of jail since I was 8 years old.

High School Graduation Me & Daddy

My prom

College Trunk Party My mentor, Ms Erica, and I

### "According to statistics, I should have been an alcoholic."

My mom's husband, Daddy, was the glue that kept everything together. He took care of my 5 siblings and I when my mom was away, and as you can imagine, we struggled financially with only one working parent.

We were homeless a few times and lived with friends and family and in hotels.

At one point, my family of 7 even lived in a one-bedroom shelter shortly after my older sister ran away from home in high school.

I'm a firm believer that no pain lasts forever and there's always a light at the end of the dark tunnel.

For me, that light came when I was 17 years old. Little did I know, the light was short-lived and I'd find myself back in the tunnel searching for my way out sooner than I had expected.

# The Day My Life Changed Forever

Do you ever feel like obstacles are always being thrown your way? It's like you take two steps forward and get pushed back 5 steps.

That's how I felt most of the time but let me tell you- when I turned 17, life had finally gotten better.

By this time, my relationship with my mom had gotten better (I'll tell you more about how we got there later), my family had our own apartment, and we were somewhat normal.

Though we lived in the hood, we had our own, and that's what was important.

# So picture this...

I'm a senior in high school. I have a job, I'm applying to colleges and I'm preparing for prom. You can't tell me nothing!

In May, I graduate from high school and I receive an acceptance letter to a small college in Pennsylvania that's close enough to home in case I need money or get homesick, but far enough where I don't have to worry about anybody sneaking up on me when I'm trying to TURN UP! Ya girl is going to Kutztown University.

In addition to all the other good stuff that's happening in my life, I'm also preparing for a church missionary trip to Trinidad and Tobago. Have you ever been outside of the country? This would be my first time and I'm so excited!

Trinidad and Tobago is an island in the Caribbean that's known for its beautiful climate and rich culture. I was chosen to go on this trip to help developing communities and learn more about religion and spirituality.

Since I have to leave for the trip from Virginia, my mom and Daddy make our little road trip a family affair. The plan is, my parents and siblings would take me to Virginia to see me off and get a mini vacay out of the deal; two birds, one stone.

# Let the countdown begin!

Before I leave for the trip, I'm making sure that everything is ready for college because I start college a few weeks after I return home.

The day before I leave I'm on the computer talking to my future roommate trying to figure out who's gonna bring the micro-fridge, how much space we'll have, and what we'll do the night we arrive. Out of nowhere, Daddy calls out my name and asks, "Terri, can you go get my bag from the kitchen?"

I didn't respond right away because I had a little attitude, but thought to myself, "Daddy, I'm 17, I'm going to college and my life is lit. Don't nobody got time for that." I was so irked, okay?

I looked at him, he looked at me, and then he said, "It's cool I got it."

I went back to emailing my future roommate trying to figure out if she knew any boys at the school and where the parties were. I happened to look over and saw Daddy limping to the kitchen. I felt kind of bad for not getting his bag. Ya know? You ever treat your parents like crap and feel badly about it later? Yea, that was me!

**"Butterflies instantly fill my stomach as tears gush out of my eyes like waterfalls."**

It's July 20th, the day before my big trip and my mom, Daddy, and 4 younger siblings and I pull up to the Days Inn hotel in Harrisonburg, Virginia. My mom and I take turns driving since Daddy isn't feeling too well.

My Family

After a 5 hour drive from Chester, PA, I'm ready to get away from my brothers and sisters (ages 3, 4, 5 and 10. Yes, my parents had their hands full!) They're driving me crazy! Daddy and I walk up to the hotel receptionist. I notice that Daddy was in pain and barely able to speak to the lady behind the counter, so I assist him as any good daughter would.

I give the lady his information and read off his confirmation number as he slouches over on the desk trying to regain his balance. We get in the room, settle down and the fussing and obnoxiousness begins.

My brothers and sisters are unusually rowdy and I'm just not in the mood. As they hop around the room chasing each other around I think of a way to convince my mom into letting me stay with my friends in a different hotel.

Though my siblings are annoying me, I am super excited for tomorrow. It's the day I begin my missionary trip which includes a 3-week project in Trinidad and Tobago. I mean, what 17-year-old wouldn't be psyched for this once in a lifetime opportunity?

By the way, my plan works! I talk my mom into dropping me off at my friend Juju's hotel, which is up the street from where my family is staying. Before I rush out the door, I look back, and see Daddy lying down half asleep while my little brother is sitting behind him attempting to play peek-a-boo, and my other three siblings are roaming around. I walk over to Daddy, give him a kiss and whisper "I love you."

# July 21, 2007

My friends and I have an epic girls night the day before our big trip. Juju and I are both going to Trinidad and Tobago so her foster mom, Mrs. Joan, is going to drop us off together in the morning.

On July 21, 2007, we wake up, start prepping our bags and get in a circle for a quick prayer for traveling mercy. We always do this before any big trips to calm our nerves and put out good energy for the journey.

Mrs. Joan gets a phone call shortly after our prayer. She's on the phone for less than a minute when she screams at the top of her lungs.

The day we arrived to Trinidad & Tobago

Butterflies instantly fill my stomach as tears gush out of my eyes like waterfalls. You ever get that feeling in your stomach where you know something bad has happened or it's about to happen? That's exactly how I feel.

I listen to Mrs. Joan's reaction to figure out what's going on. You won't believe what happened. I can't believe what happened. Daddy just passed away in the hotel room in front of my mom and 4 younger siblings.

Me and Amani eating lunch with friends in Trinidad

I'm usually super self-conscious and reserved, but after hearing the news, I'm in shock. I carelessly run outside the hotel room pushing past strangers until I make my way into the empty parking lot.

I look up at the sky, hands outstretched, tears flowing down my face, and cry out, "Why, God? Why me? What did I do to deserve this?"

The rest of the day is pretty much a blur. What seemed like hundreds of phone calls are made to family and friends to update them on the tragic news.

My pastors and other close family friends drive down from Philadelphia to meet my now-widowed mom and her 5 children in Virginia to help out and guide us through this crazy situation.

There's so much going on, and while everyone is trying to play it cool and make things less awkward, there's a dark cloud hovering over us because we're all trying to process what just happened.

The head of our household, my strong, funny, supportive, and super corny dad... isn't here. He's gone forever, just like that. The glue that kept us together for all these years has dissolved, and I don't think anyone knows what to do. I sure don't.

## "Why couldn't you just get his freakin' bag from the kitchen?"

I remember sitting in the back of my mentor's car as her and her husband drove me to the university where I was supposed to get dropped off for this trip; I was bawling my eyes out.

I just wanted to see Daddy again and hug him. Even if he was dead, I just wanted to be with him.

I felt like I owed him an apology. I kept asking myself, "Why couldn't you just get his freakin' bag from the kitchen the day before you left when he asked you to?" That was literally the last thing he asked me to do, and I was so selfish.

I beat myself up about this for a long time. I sat in the back seat for what felt like hours, and just kept replaying the past few days with Daddy. I had so much regret and guilt on my shoulders. *Why didn't I treat him better when he was here?*

My future also flashed before my eyes and I thought about the trip, college, and my family. *How would I make it? What am I going to do?*

# 2 hours later...

My mentor, Mrs. Renee, hands me tissues while I flood her backseat with my uncontrollable sobbing.

As we drive to the university, she gently whispers, "It's okay to cry, it's okay to be upset, just don't give up."

I'm not ready to receive what she's saying, but I don't forget it either.

What was supposed to be one of the best days of my life quickly turned into the most devastating day for my family and I. I really don't know how I'm going to survive this.

# an hour later...

As we pull up to Eastern Mennonite University's campus in Harrisonburg, Virginia, I see my family and friends hanging out next to one of the university buildings.

I get myself together as much as I can, embrace my family, and greet my friends.

My mom and I meet with the university staff and learn that I won't be able to attend both this once-in-a-lifetime missions trip and Daddy's funeral because of the travel schedule.

As a 17-years-old, I have to make one of the most difficult decisions in my life. Do I attend this amazing missions trip where I can help less fortunate people plant gardens and accomplish their personal goals, or do I attend Daddy's funeral?

I think long and hard about Daddy and his personality and about what he'd say if he were here, "Girl, you better go on that trip. We raised all that money for you to get this far. We don't have money like that. You're not missing anything at home."

My mom also reassured me, "Baby girl, this is your decision to make and no one else's. I support whatever you want to do." One of the camp counselors also came to me and told me to think about how I would feel about the decision I make today, 5 years from now. That helped a lot!

With the help of my support system, I was empowered to make the decision I felt comfortable with. I did the thing I thought my future self (adult Terri) would appreciate and not regret. Some people judged me for it, while others said I was brave.

I decided to go on the trip. The day my dad died, I left my family and I embarked on my first missions trip with an amazing group of people.

**"I did the thing I thought my future self (the adult Terri) would appreciate and not regret. Some people judged me for it. While others said I was brave."**

Looking back on that experience as an adult still makes me emotional. I'm literally crying as I'm writing this, mostly because I still miss Daddy like crazy and writing my story is like reliving the experience all over again. But I have no regrets outside of how I treated him when he was alive, of course.

Even though I missed Daddy's funeral, the 3 weeks I spent on the missions trip was the best environment for me to be in at that critical time in my life.

I had a chance to make a new friend, Amani, who said that she was so inspired by the fact that I was on that trip, considering I lost my dad the same day. We became great friends and helped each other through some tough times that we experienced after the trip.

I did a speech in front of all the camp counselors and other students on the trip. It was so dope to be able to tell them about Daddy and what he taught me about life.

I made an impact in Trinidad and Tobago and had plenty of quiet time to write and reflect. I even wrote Daddy a letter to express how I felt about him, which gave me a lot of closure.

Looking back on that experience, I realize that being on that trip provided me with a healing space and a supportive group of people that my home life could not have provided me with. Today, I'm so proud of the decision that 17-year-old Terri made.

*Lemons -*
*Lemons represent the sour or difficult circumstances we experience in life. Daddy's death was a lemon as was the abuse I experienced. But a lemon doesn't have to be tragic or extremely "dramatic," it's anything that causes pain, heartbreak or a challenge for you. A lemon could be struggling with a learning disability or breaking up with a good friend.*

# Chapter 2
# The Big Pitcher

**In this book, we're going to talk all about making lemonade, overcoming adversity, and creating a road-map for the life of your dreams.**

Before we dive into any of that, we must talk about the pitcher... the Big Pitcher, that is.

Before you do anything with the lemons life has given you, you have to find a pitcher for the lemonade you'll make, right?

Now in the real world, the pitcher represents your solid support system or your squad. Who are the people that will root for you when you're succeeding, hold you when you fall, and give you a shoulder to cry on when it gets tough or when squeezing your lemons becomes painful?

I used to always want to do things on my own because my life circumstances demanded that I be independent. I had to learn that it's

***The Pitcher*** *- The pitcher represents your support system. The people who will give you a shoulder to cry on as you "make lemonade." These are the people who will hold you and nurture you as you grow and make progress. Sometimes we may outgrow our current pitchers and need to pour our lemonade into a new pitcher based on where we are in life, and that's okay.*

**The Lemonade** - In order to make lemonade, we have to squeeze the lemons. Squeezing can relieve stress and provide therapeutic benefits but sometimes you can get lemon juice in your eyes or the eyes of those around you. This makes the process painful and sometimes risky. That's why we need a solid pitcher. Making lemonade is defined as digging deep down within to find a positive moment, an opportunity, or a lesson from a seemingly bad or painful situation. We'll talk more about this later.

**The sugar** - Sometimes you need to add sugar to make your lemonade taste better. Sugar represents your own personal development, the shifts in your perspective that'll allow you to see a bigger vision for your life, and steps to heal yourself on the journey. The sugar empowers you to go from bitterness to betterness.

**Stir and add water** - Stirring and adding water represents the fact that you'll be shaking things up a bit in both your life and the lives of others as you make lemonade. You'll need some valuable nuggets of wisdom in order to successfully make lemonade and dilute the sour taste of lemons. We'll dive into the tips you'll need in a later chapter.

**Make Lemonade and Share It** - You have something unique to offer the world - and you don't need to be perfect, or shout your personal business from the rooftops, to do so. All you need to do is show up as the person you needed when you were younger and to share your experiences with others - perhaps it's the kids in your community, the students at your school, coworkers at your job or maybe even your cousins or siblings that look up to you. When we share our stories, we liberate others to acknowledge and validate their stories.

okay to lean on people, ask for help, and let my squad support me.

## Your vibe attracts your tribe

Many times, my parents weren't available to help me throughout my journey. In those moments, I depended on my grandparents, pastors, mentors, teachers, friends, and other positive people that truly wanted the best for me.

Think about the type of people you want around you. What kind of vibe do they have? How do they make you feel?

Do they promote positive change, or do they suck your energy and leave you feeling less than?

There's a saying that goes, "you are the average of the five people you spend the most time with." It's true!

Think about it: successful people hang around successful people. If you want to achieve a particular goal, slowly begin adding people to your support system or friend group who've already achieved (or who are on their way towards) that goal. That way, you can all inspire one another, instead of dragging each other down.

## No new friends?

Ever since I started school, my mom was adamant about providing feedback on anyone I tried to befriend. She'd be like "Mmm, I don't like her. Watch out for that girl," or "I get a bad vibe from him. You'll see."

Even though my mom got on my nerves with this, she was onto something because most of the time... she was right! Moms be knowin'.

A lot of the kids my age that were "lit", were also getting into trouble, and while I'm not telling you how to choose your friends, I am encouraging you to watch the people you hang around. Remember that when someone shows you who they are, believe them and don't try to make excuses for them.

You know who's best for you, and who means you no good. Trust your gut!

**"You stifle your potential if you don't utilize the resources and people around you..."**

When I look back over my life, there are so many situations I can think of where I needed someone to support me because I couldn't handle it on my own.

An example is the time I was spiraling into a deep dark depression because my crush wasn't as into me as I was into him. My best friend, Amina, helped me get my mind right and gave me what I couldn't give myself: unbiased advice I had trouble seeing through my heart-filled eyes.

Or the time when I went for my first pap smear and my mom couldn't come with me because she was locked up. Would you believe that I saw one of my mentors in the waiting room who gave me some encouragement and made me feel less nervous about the whole ordeal?

I also think about my high school days when I was taking those SAT prep classes, writing college application essays, trying to narrow down my options and oh, don't forget about trying to figure out how the hell to complete the FAFSA. OMG!

In those moments, I went to my high school guidance counselor, Mr. Pomarico, because my family didn't really know much about the process.

# Who's in your corner?

I used to think that asking for help was weak, but I quickly learned that smart people speak up and ask for what they need. Every single successful person you know had someone in their corner and has a team to help them.

I also learned to get advice from people who are where I want to be. If I want to learn how to play basketball, I'm not going to go to my friend that plays soccer. I'll probably hit up my home boy that balls, so he can teach me from his first-hand experience.

Finding a support system of good people who believe in you and positive friends that want the best for you is going to be so important, not just for your personal journey, but also for the rest of this book.

# Finding your Pitcher

## 1. Who's in your corner?

**A)** I want you to take a step back, zoom out of your life and pretend to be looking down at your life from a bird's eye-view. Think about the people in your life that you spend most of your time with. Whether we choose to be around them or they're in our lives by default, we all have people in our corner. Just because someone is there and you have access to each other, doesn't mean they'll have a positive impact. Right now we're only focused on getting a better idea of who's around you. In column A, list the names of each person you spend a lot of time with. You may want to draw a line and write each person on their respective line to make the next step in the activity easier.

**B) In column B, across from each person's name, write down how that person makes you feel most of the time. Be honest - no judgment and no excuses. You got this!**

A)

B)

## 2. Think about how you like to feel.

For example, I like to be happy, positive, funny, creative, clutter-free and free-spirited. I also don't like to be around sad stuff, drama, and injustice. Since I have a clear idea on what I like and don't like, it makes it easy for me to choose what types of people I'm around, in addition to who's in my squad or who's part of my pitcher. Use the space below to answer the following questions.

**How do I like to feel?**

**What feelings don't I like?**

**Based on what you've shared above, think about the people who are in your corner that bring about the vibes you're looking for and the feelings you enjoy feeling. Write their names below.**

These people are your new and improved support system. They are your pitcher! If you don't think you have enough, add a few wishlist people you'd love to have in your corner and think of how you might provide that person with value in exchange for their support. Maybe you're good at computers, or maybe you can help them with social media or filing paperwork. When you look to provide value to others and you believe in yourself, they'll be more likely to support you.

## Having a hard time finding your Pitcher?

There were times in my journey when I didn't feel as though I had a solid pitcher so I would adopt mentors in my head. I would read self-help books and professional development books from people I admire. You don't necessarily need to have access to someone in order to get support and encouragement from them. Yes, it's ideal but you can also read their books, follow them on social media, invest in their products or services, etc... These are all ways that we can cultivate more of what we want in our lives when we're seeking support.

# Chapter 3
# The Main Squeeze

**I grew up in a household where I often heard the phrase, "What happens in this house, stays in this house." Can you relate?**

Basically what this meant was, don't be telling anyone our family business, no matter how good, bad, painful, or blissful that business is... and I followed this advice for a long time.

I was molested and physically abused when I was little and didn't tell anyone for years because of the saying I grew up with.

I learned how to hide my true feelings so well that I could walk into a room with a smile so bright that no one would know that I was hurting on the inside, crying on the inside, and desperately wishing I could let someone inside. I needed help.

The only way I knew to cope with what happened to me was to push that stuff so far down and sort of pretend like it didn't happen. I ignored and denied my truth, even though it'd randomly pop up in my mind like I was replaying a movie I had seen at a theater. My past haunted me but I didn't know how to make it go away.

## "...in my eyes, becoming an adult would make everything better.."

As a teenager, my number one priority was to grow up, move out of the house, get my own car, and live life my way. I figured being grown and finally reaching adulthood would solve all my problems and make the bad things that happened go away.

Life required me to grow up fast. I didn't have an issue with that because in my eyes, becoming an adult would make everything better.

The gag is, once I got all grown, got my car, graduated from college, earned my degrees, and started making a lot more money... I realized that the things that happened to me when I was younger never really left me. I grew up but I didn't truly glow up internally. Sometimes it felt like my 10-year-old self was living in a grown-up body. I was still afraid, depressed, hurt, and insecure.

No matter how much money I made, how many accomplishments I achieved or how amazing my relationship was, there was work within myself that needed to be done... and no one else could do the work but me.

## "You can't heal what you don't reveal!"

I started journaling and being honest with myself about what happened to me. Yes, it was painful but it was so necessary. Today, I'm grateful I started that healing process because it allowed me to be a better me: a better student, sister, daughter, wife, businesswoman and person.

It answered a lot of questions I had and made it easier to forgive myself. You know how hard it is to forgive ourselves sometimes.

Here's an example: I used to be very shy, timid, and fearful. I was afraid of everything. I used to flinch when people would make fast movements near me, and cower in fear. I was afraid to speak up in class and raise my hand. I was self-conscious and uncomfortable in my own skin.

I hated the fact that I was so "weak", as I used to call it. I admired my classmates who were bold and fearless. They'd unapologetically say what's on their mind and do what

they wanted to do. I, on the other hand, felt like a pushover.

But then I took the time to reflect on my journey, and I realized "Wait, I'm an abuse survivor." Those characteristics and actions (being shy, timid and flinching often) kept me safe at one point in my life. They served me well and I needed them when I was being abused; being uncomfortable in my skin made me hyper-observant, so if I was about to be attacked, I'd be prepared to cover myself. You know what I mean?

Some of us have faced really tough situations in life which made us a certain way, and we're so hard on ourselves when we should really be thanking ourselves for doing what we needed to do to keep us safe at that point. The next goal is to develop new characteristics that will serve us today.

# CAUTION: Squeezing in progress

This might be a little refresher but it's important to revisit, so let's dig in.

Making lemonade is defined as digging deep down within to find a positive moment, an opportunity, or a lesson from a seemingly bad or painful situation. In order to make lemonade, we have to squeeze the lemons, which is what we're about to do here.

Squeezing our lemons requires honesty about what happened to us, where we are in our lives, and how what happened impacted us. It's sort of like you analyzing your challenges.

Just like squeezing a stress ball can relieve stress and provide therapeutic benefits, squeezing your lemons can do the same, but sometimes you can get lemon juice in your eyes or the eyes of those around you. This makes the process painful and sometimes risky. That's why we need a solid pitcher.

## What do you think?

In the next few pages, I'm going to squeeze some of my lemons and I want you to think about how I was able to overcome them.

What characteristics do you see me exhibiting in my story, and how might you use them for your own lemons?

Who am I depending on, and what feelings do I feel at each stage in my journey?

## The Other F Word

I've always viewed forgiveness as an extremely limited and narrow process.

In theory, I'd give each person I met a "forgiveness allotment" which, depending on the nature of the relationship, would abide by the three strikes law. If someone betrayed me more than 3 times, they got cut off-period.

Occasionally I'd cut someone off before their 3rd strike, but more often than not, I'd give an individual 3 times to mess up before I withdrew from the relationship. In my mind, it made sense, and if and when I betrayed someone, I expected the same thing.

**One relationship that continues to test my ability to forgive is the relationship that I have with my mom.**

I thought my method kept me safe. However, a few months ago, I was challenged to revisit my philosophy on forgiveness.

My mom has been in and out of jail since I was 8 years old. I won't go into detail about why she went away out of respect for her story and personal journey but a few years ago, she was sentenced to 4 years in prison, the longest consecutive amount of time that she's ever done.

For the majority of my undergraduate career and some of the most important years of my younger siblings' lives, my mom was locked up.

I figured that after this 4-year stint, my mom would get her act together and tap into her potential! I just knew that she would change after being away from us for so long.

Unfortunately, less than a year after she was released, my mom was back in the same predicament. She was arrested for the same crime that put her away 4 years earlier.

Words can't even describe how I felt. All I know is that I found myself on the familiar road to forgiveness that I thought was over.

I felt that I had given all that I was capable of giving without losing myself. I DID NOT want to forgive anymore. I was tired. I was hurt. I was angry. I was confused. It was unfair. I couldn't fathom how someone could continue to make decisions that would take them away from their family.

Yes, we all make mistakes and I'm guilty of doing wrong to others, but I just couldn't get past this one.

**After sharing my story with a few supportive friends, I was challenged to forgive.**

I knew what I needed to do, but I really didn't know how. This situation hurt me to the core.

I mean, it was the kind of hurt where you see other mothers and daughters, and you're slightly envious because you wish that your mother-daughter relationship was better.

It was the kind of hurt where you love someone so much, but you don't know how to move past their actions without hurting yourself. It was the kind of hurt that made you tear up in public at the thought of the mundane.

It was the kind of hurt that NEEDED me to forgive.

**Below are 4 realizations that assisted me (and continue to do so) with the never ending process of forgiveness:**

# 1. Be Empathetic

Put yourself in the other person's shoes. In this case, it'd be the person who hurt you or offended you. Hear me out on this one before you start SYH (Shaking Your Head.) Learn about their life, learn about what has caused them to act the way that they act, and think about what that person has been through.

Whether you've been abused, misused, cheated on, or disrespected, seeing things from the other person's point of view may be difficult because you are taking the attention off of yourself and viewing the situation from a different perspective. This step is challenging but also very, very important. I must admit, viewing the situation from an empathetic point of view is going to require you to be open-minded, objective, and mature. It's no joke, but it is worth it.

After talking to my mom and grandmother, I learned that my mom has been through her own struggles that I don't even think I would have been able to survive.

Now let me tell you, being empathetic is not a way to justify anyone's behavior. Yes, the person who hurt you was wrong, and you did not deserve to be hurt. Your feelings are valid and you are entitled to them. Being empathetic allows you to be more understanding. It gives you more compassion and insight. Once I learned more about my mom's past, it gave me clarity as to how she could have made some of the bad decisions that she made.

Let's think about it in a way that my pastor explained it to me when I was a teen. Let's say that everyone has an invisible shelf. Come on, use your

imagination, I'm going somewhere with this. This figurative shelf is nothing more than a person's essence. We all have items on our shelves: values, morals, personality traits and other qualities that make us who we are. What's on an individual's shelf is largely influenced by their upbringing, life experiences, society, and other factors.

## Let's say Random Cute Guy meets Random Cute Girl and they hit it off.

At some point in their relationship, many of those shelf items will be "exposed." Sometimes we look for things in people, and become disappointed because what we look for is simply not on that individual's shelf- whether it be affection, love, attention, gratification or any other "thing" that we look for in a person. This causes us to be bitter and unforgiving because we didn't get what we felt we deserved.

If you look at Random Cute Guy's shelf though, we can see that he was abused and also struggles with low self-esteem. We can be empathetic by understanding how and why he may be abusive and negative. At the same time, we may want to remove ourselves from that relationship because of his traits, forgive him and ourselves, and keep it pushing.

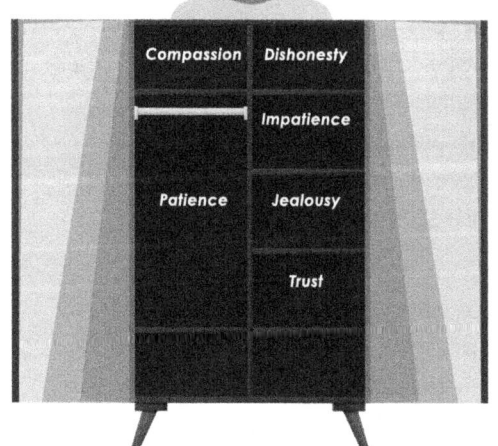

If we bring this back to empathy and forgiveness, I can see what's on my mom's shelf based on past experience. Now when she shows up displaying what's on her shelf, let's say it's a lack of patience, I'm not as impacted because I know her nature and how to remove myself from the situation if need be. If patience isn't on someone's shelf, we shouldn't be as surprised when they fail to display patience.

**"Forgiveness is like accounting- you have to balance the books. You have to come to a conclusion about your life, or you'll be miserable for the rest of your life. In the process of balancing the books, you have to get an understanding not only of your situation, but the knowledge that this person could not give you what they didn't have. Just because you wanted it doesn't mean they had it in the warehouse of their personality to complete the inventory of your need."**

-Paraphrased quote by Bishop T.D. Jakes

## 2. Take Off the Victim Badge

Oftentimes, when someone does us wrong, it hurts us to the core. Some of us walk around with a chip on our shoulder or a badge of victimization. Wearing a victim badge is like walking around flaunting our heartache and using it as an excuse.

When we're wearing this "badge", our thought process may sound like: "I was abused when I was younger so the world owes me something" or "This one guy hurt me so now I'm going to use any other guy I meet" or "I was teased and everyone said I was dumb, so I guess I'll just drop out because I don't have any other choice."

Sometimes we put demands on people who had nothing to do with the hurt and pain that we feel, but that's not fair because we're setting ourselves up for failure. No matter what we've been through, the world doesn't owe us anything and neither does anyone else. We owe it to ourselves to let go of the victim mentality.

The first step I took in taking off my victim badge was acknowledgment. "Yes I was abused. Yes I was hurt. Yes, I was abandoned. Yes, the experiences

that I had, were painful and they made me bitter."

Your feelings and emotions are all valid. It's important to realize that you were betrayed. Someone took advantage of you or hurt you, and it wasn't right. In order for you to overcome, you must vow to be a victor instead of a victim. You cannot let your circumstances define how far you go in life. As painful as it may be, you can't let that define your attitude toward life or other innocent bystanders. If you want to overcome, you must have a victorious attitude, and that all starts in the mind. Saying things like: "I will be okay" or "I am an overcomer" and "I will keep pressing!" are statements that will help with your victorious mentality. We'll dive a bit deeper into this in the following chapters.

## 3. Refocus Your Energy

There are times when I look back over my life and all that I've experienced and I become angry. I regret not being given certain opportunities. I regret some of the decisions that I made, and quite frankly, I'm tempted to take my anger out on others.

Over the years, I've learned to refocus that negative energy and I've learned to view failure, negativity and anything that isn't good for me as my enemy instead of taking that anger out on others. This perspective prevents me from proactively using the energy to fight against someone who's done harm to me or an innocent bystander.

When bad things happen, when someone does me wrong, when a door is slammed in my face, I fight against failure and the negative emotions as if it were a person who's trying to hold me back. In situations like these, I try to keep the focus on me. I ask myself, "This person did me wrong, but what must I do to continue on the path to success?" It's easier said than done, but it has really helped me to overcome.

## 4. Remember That You're Forgiving for Yourself

I always looked at forgiveness as "letting the other person off the hook", but in reality, we forgive for ourselves. If you want a better life for yourself, it's important to forgive. No one wants to walk around with bitterness or a victim complex. Another humble reminder is that there are times when we need to be forgiven, so it's only right that we forgive others.

Walking around with unforgiveness and bitterness is like drinking poison and expecting the other person to die. Oftentimes, the person that hurt us is out living their best life, but

we are the ones with the burden of bitterness on our shoulders weighing us down heavily and impacting our lives negatively.

These steps may sound simple, but it's a process. There may be some tears. It'll take time. But forgiveness is a necessary process. For the best results, use these tips when you are not emotionally charged.

When I first found out that my mom got locked up again, I was not in the right space to use these steps. I was too angry, upset and ultimately too emotionally unstable to consider forgiveness right off the bat. I knew that I needed to forgive my mom, but I just wasn't ready or willing to walk through this process. I had to give myself a window of time to vent, be angry, cry and get all of my negative and natural emotions out. Once my emotions died down, I revisited these steps because I knew that was the only way I could live a healthy and happy life.

It's also important to note that you can forgive someone and choose to remove them from your life, especially if they continue to violate you and disregard your boundaries.

My cohost and I had a chance to interview Dr. Thema Bryant-Davis, a multi-talented professor and author, on our podcast, H.E.R Space, and she shared a beautiful quote about forgiveness.

**"I can forgive someone and still not hang around them. I can forgive someone who is not sorry but I can only be reconciled with someone who is authentically, truly repentant and transformed so that I do not continue to be exposed to trauma."**

- Dr. Thema Bryant-Davis

# Let's chat!

## Reflect on my story, think about your personal experiences, and answer the questions below.

**Who hurt you?**




**How did this hurt impact you?**




**What characteristics and life experiences are on this person's shelf?**




**How can you forgive this person(s)? What does forgiving this person look like?**

# Dear Mama: Standing Up to My Mom for the First Time

When I turned 18, I didn't feel like a woman and I sure didn't feel like an adult. I felt like the same little girl who was punched in the face by her mom in the 5th grade for having a messy desk and writing a love note to a little boy in her class.

I felt like the same little girl who cowered in the presence of people who were outspoken and more confident than her.

I felt like the same little girl who lived in silence for fear of offending, upsetting, or disagreeing with someone else's opinion.

**Despite growing up in an abusive household, I thought that when I turned 18 something magical would happen.**

I assumed the world would naturally respect me, and treat me like the adult and woman I longed to be. But they didn't.

It was my sophomore year of college, and I was stressed. In addition to staying on top of my academics, finding money for school and trying to maintain my social life, I found myself driving home nearly every weekend to take my siblings to church, or to drive them 4 1/2 hours to visit my mom in prison.

One weekend while I was home, I got a call from my mom. She called asking if I could bring my siblings to see her, call one of her friends, and do a few other favors for her. I've always been intimidated by my mom. She is the definition of a strong, black woman.

Although she had stopped being abusive when I was in high school, her words were still powerful and captivating enough that when she spoke- whether positively or negatively- her words could either mend a broken heart or pierce it. When my mom asked me to do a few favors for her, I responded in a way that was foreign to me. I said "No."

With a river of tears streaming down my face, I whined, "No, I don't want to bring them up and I'm not going to. I've done so much and I have so much on my plate. I don't feel like it, mom."

I couldn't believe it! Those three seemingly small sentences were the biggest sentences of my life! I finally said "No"! I said it respectably, but I still didn't go along with what she wanted mo to do. I chose to put myself first. I had a busy workload, I didn't have the money, and it was too much for me.

**I've always been a people pleaser, a push-over, a hopeless chameleon who conformed to the views of others.**

As a child, my opinion never mattered and the abuse I had gone through magnified my unworthiness. I felt like I didn't exist. I was merely a reflection of everyone that I encountered. I had no opinion, no thoughts, no mind of my own.

However, the day that I said "No" to my mom was the day that I started fighting for myself. It was the day that I felt like I was finally becoming a woman. My mom sounded shocked and disgusted by this new word that I had learned, and abruptly ended our phone conversation.

I cried hysterically in my grandfather's arms. He supported me, held me, and let me have the space I needed to cry, stand in my truth, and morph into the independent woman I was meant to be.

# Standing Up to My Mom for the First Time

Although I was vulnerable, I felt like I was finally on my way to becoming a big girl. I followed up that prison call with a long letter explaining how I felt to my mom. One of the most significant paragraphs from that letter was:

**"Mom, you are a strong black woman. You're outspoken and independent.**

**Unfortunately, I wasn't given the opportunity to be this way. I was always being shut down and suppressed, and I never had my own opinion because I was so used to agreeing with you in order to avoid conflict.**

**I never know if I'm sad, mad or happy because after denying my feelings for so long, when I feel a bad emotion, I feel guilty and suppress it."**

Whew! I'm getting emotional just replaying these events! I don't remember how my mom responded to the letter, but I do know that after the letter, we didn't talk for some time.

It took us a while to rekindle our relationship, and when we did, it was like meeting each other for the first time. We had a newfound respect for each other. During our time apart, I focused on forgiving my mom for her mistakes. It was a painful, but necessary prerequisite to healing. I also began reinventing myself.

I had conformed to those around me for so long that by this stage in my life, I felt like a baby. I felt like I was starting from scratch. It was challenging, yet sobering.

It gave me the opportunity to figure out what womanhood meant to me, along with identifying what kind of woman I wanted to become. Some of the characteristics I wanted to possess were confidence, humility, determination, assertiveness, independence, and positivity.

Over the past few years, I've been able to transform from the timid and fearful young girl I once was, into a strong black woman. Who would have ever thought?

# Dear Mama: Standing Up to My Mom for the First Time Reflection

I'm going to dissect the story you just read, and answer the questions below because these are tough questions. You'll have a chance to answer the questions after.

As you read my feedback below, think about this whole process. How does it feel? What's coming to mind for you? Remember this because you'll be going through a similar process for the lemons in your life very soon.

If you find that your answers differ from mine, that's okay. We may have different perspectives about my situation. You may see something I missed, and I might enlighten you to a new view you haven't considered. See what feels right to you while also leaning into my story to better understand how I was feeling.

**What was my lemon?** My lemon is my lack of confidence and assertiveness. The lack of these traits kept me safe

when I was younger. If I had displayed too much confidence or assertiveness as a child, I could have gotten in much more trouble and **the abuse could have been worse.**

**How did this lemon impact me?** Well first of all, this lemon kept me safe. As an adult, I thank little Terri, my younger self, for doing what she needed to do to keep me from experiencing more pain and hurt as a child. Wow! Talk about being a strong kid. As a teen and adult, these traits didn't help me much. My lack of confidence caused me to tolerate a lot of B.S. in relationships. I was an easy target for people interested in taking advantage of others.

Lacking assertiveness also made it easy for people to treat me like a pushover, and I often found myself in situations where I asked myself, "How the hell did I get here?"

**What did we learn when I squeezed (or examined) the lemon?** Although I had never said "No" to my mom, I actually had the strength and power within me to do it, I just had to take the first step. I had to try, even if it was through tears and a shaky voice.

Sometimes in life, you have to say no to someone else in order to say yes to yourself. People won't always like it when you speak up for yourself, but what's most important is being true to yourself and what you believe to be your truth. I was bummed out that my mom and I weren't on good terms, but after I said no to her, it made it easier for me to say no to bad relationships that weren't good for me, friendships that didn't give as much as I was giving, and situations that didn't feel good. When you speak your truth, you sleep better at night.

**What characteristics did I display?** I think I displayed some **critical thinking skills.** I thought about the dynamic that my mom and I had, and when she asked me to do something I thought was unreasonable, I decided to question the norm because it didn't make sense. This is key.

Sometimes we find ourselves doing things out of obligation or because we've always done them, and it becomes second-nature. We don't question why we do it or if we enjoy doing it, we just do it because we've always done it. On the day my mom asked me to run errands and push myself more than I could offer, I spoke up for myself. I displayed **assertiveness** like I never have before. There's a quote that says, "You tell the world how to treat you by what you allow." The day I spoke up for myself, I let my mom know that I have boundaries.

You can't just tell me what to do, but instead you can ask me to do a favor and I'll let you know if it works for me. Being respectful to my elders is important to me, and I also ask that my elders respect me as well.

We both deserve respect and that's what I communicated to my mom that day.

Who was my pitcher (or the person I depended on)? In this situation, my grandfather, affectionately known as Poppop, was my pitcher. He supported me, and provided comfort during this difficult shift in power between my mom and I.

**BONUS: How did I make lemonade? Well, I'm sharing my story and tips with you. This is sort of a trick question but after squeezing my lemon (or analyzing the situation), I found a way to share my story to help others on a similar path of finding their voice and speaking up for themselves.**

Personal Reflection - Dear Mama: Standing Up to My Mom for the First Time

# Let's chat!

## Answer the questions below on your own and refer to the previous page if you need some guidance.

**What was my lemon?**

**How did this lemon impact me?**

**What did we learn when I squeezed (or examined the lemon)?**

**What characteristics did I display?**

**Who was my pitcher (or the person I depended on)?**

**What could I have done differently?**

## BONUS: How did I make lemonade?

# Match the Struggle to the Win

On the following page, draw a line to connect each lemon with the appropriate sliced lemon. Next, draw a line to connect the sliced lemon with the appropriate glass of lemonade.

Mari Copeny and her community are fighting a life-threatening water crisis in Flint, Michigan.

I was upset by the lack of visitors and family members caring for the elderly.

I wrote a letter to President Obama about the water system in my city and he met with me and later authorized $100 million to repair Flint's water system.

Abigail Lupi visits her great-grandma in a nursing home to sing a song for her 100th birthday and realizes how lonely the elderly are there.

I was misunderstood. I was bullied. I had something to get off my chest based on what I experienced.

I joined the Florida Immigrant Coalition and helped others like me navigate changes in policies and the emotional turmoil of possibly being deported.

Julio Calderon is experiencing violence in his home country and decides to take his siblings and cross the Mexican border into the United States for safety.

I am undocumented. I came to the U.S. when I was 16. I did not benefit from DACA.

12 people died from exposure to bacteria in the water in Flint between 2014-2015.

Almost 100,000 people in my city are drinking contaminated water.

I created positive videos on social media to share my story and it went viral. Then I became a motivational speaker and traveled around the world to share my message about confidence and self-love.

Nyeeam Hudson is playing in a park when other kids start teasing him about his outdated sneakers.

I started CareGirlz, a troupe of kids who spend their free time visiting aged care homes and hospitals to perform for, and chat with, the elderly. We've brightened the day of more than 1,000 people so far.

# Match the Struggle to the Win - Answer Key

"Mari Copeny, **an 11-year-old** with an irrepressible desire to make the world a better place, is remarkable proof that you're never too young to be an activist.

Copeny, also known as "Little Miss Flint," is an advocate for her hometown of Flint, Michigan, which has been fighting a life threatening water crisis since 2014. When she was **8 years old**, she penned a powerful letter to President Obama on behalf of Flint and its children who could no longer drink from the tap, shower without their eyes burning, or even safely use a Slip 'N Slide.

Obama replied to Copeny, visited Flint, and eventually signed off on $100 million in funding to help repair the city's poisoned water system. But Copeny wasn't done advocating for change." - Mashable

"It was a visit to her grandma's nursing home to sing a song for her 100th birthday, which opened **10-year-old** Abigail Lupi's eyes to the loneliness faced by many elderly people in care.

Upset by the lack of visitors or family members to care for them, Abigail started CareGirlz, a troupe of talented singing, dancing and acting youngsters who spend their free time visiting aged care homes and hospitals to perform for and chat with the elderly.

A roaring success, CareGirlz has brightened the lives of over 1,000 people and is growing every year."
- Open Colleges

"**At the age of 16,** Julio Calderon made the tough decision to leave the horrors going on in his homeland of Honduras to cross the border into the United States as an unaccompanied minor. His mother was already living in the U.S., but could not petition for her kids to join her. Calderon and his siblings spent 30 days by themselves crossing the Mexican border into the U.S.

Since his arrival as an unaccompanied youth, Calderon hit the ground running with his activism for immigration reform. He's worked with the Florida Immigrant Coalition helping others like himself navigate changes in policies, as well as the emotional turmoil of the possibility of being sent back to an unstable situation in their native countries." - NBC Miami

"A few months ago, Nyeeam (NYE-eem) Hudson, at the time **10 years old**, was playing in a park in New Jersey when another child started to tease him about the outdated sneakers he was wearing.

In a now-viral cell phone video he recorded after the incident, Nyeeam pleads with parents not to raise their children to be materialistic because 'once they don't have Jordans or the cool clothes on, they're going to feel like they're not important.' Today, Nyeeam has his own brand, he's working on a book and travels around the world for speaking engagements."
- Forbes

# Let's Make Lemonade

Use the boxes below to write down a lemon or challenge you've experienced in your life in the first column. Next, use the second column to analyze each lemon and think about how it's impacted you. In the third column, I want you to make lemonade. Find a positive, a lesson, or an opportunity to turn that pain into power. If you need help, refer to the stories you read in the previous pages.

Remember, we live in a world where you can be young, old, or middle aged and still make an impact on your community and the world; age is simply a number. Also, you can pretty much Google anything these days so be sure to use your resources. Just like some of the world-changers on the previous page, I started working on my passion as a teen; I used to give speeches in church. It wasn't perfect in the beginning but it's all about progress over perfection. Happy squeezing!

# How My Siblings Saved My Life

When I was 18 years old, I found myself at home crying on my bathroom floor. I was hopeless. I was helpless. I was on the verge of giving up. I felt the weight of the world on my shoulders, and I just couldn't take it anymore. I was a sophomore in college trying to figure out how I was going to finish school.

My tuition bill was due, I was broke, and the emotions from Daddy's death were fresh and overwhelming. The one-year anniversary of his death was quickly approaching, and I was in the midst of grieving while processing my mom's new romantic relationship.

I laid on the bathroom floor sobbing uncontrollably because of the pain, but also because of what I intended to do next. I was home alone and I planned to take my life. I knew my mom had over-the-counter medicine in her medicine cabinet, and my plan was to go to her bathroom and take them all.

As I picked myself up off my bathroom floor, I heard something that stopped me in my tracks - my 4-year-old little brother's voice. He must've gotten out of school early that day. He was outside laughing and screaming and doing what kids do.

I instantly pictured him smiling from ear to ear, skipping up to the house as he often did. I thought of my siblings. *What would they do if I wasn't here? How would my decision impact them?* I thought of all the unfortunate situations that I've been through in life, and I challenged myself to muster up the strength to get over this hump. If I could just survive this hardship and make it through, I could possibly help someone else.

This was also the day that I identified my "why." I found inspiration in the following excerpt from Les Brown, one of my favorite motivational speakers:

"Suicide is a permanent solution to a temporary problem. It is the result of people convincing themselves they can't make it. In order for us to take life on even in the worst times we have to say to ourselves, 'I am going to make it no matter what.' Not making it is not an option."

## Your "why" motivates you when the going gets tough

Your "why" gets you up in the morning when you don't feel like getting up. Your "why" is that thing that inspires you, that thing that motivates you, that thing that won't let you quit! Your "why" could be your mom, dad, grandparent, siblings, niece or nephew, or your legacy. No matter how tired you are or how tough the journey has become, there is someone out there who's waiting on your victory. Your triumph alone can influence the masses.

Just think about it, if I would have taken my life that day when I was 18, I wouldn't be here to talk to you. I would have missed out on all the amazing opportunities my future afforded me because of a temporary feeling that went away. My mom and pastor helped me figure out financial aid and it was all resolved, but I would have never known that if I would have given up.

**"Suicide doesn't end the chances of life getting worse, it eliminates the possibility of it ever getting any better."**

# How My Siblings Saved My Life Reflection

Just like we did before, I'm going to analyze the story I shared with you and jot my answers down below. As you get more comfortable with squeezing my lemons and thinking about how I navigated my obstacles, try to see yourself in me and think about how you'd do the same.

There's nothing special about me and I don't possess things you can't access. Everything you need is within you and it's important that you push yourself to find the answers. Growing up, I used to think that everyone I encountered: new friends, strangers, classmates, adults, basically everyone, knew more than me, was more confident than me, and had more worth than me. This is the farthest thing from the truth and don't you forget it.

The only reason I was able to overcome the obstacles I faced is because I never gave up. I believed deep down within me that it would get better, and I was determined to live long enough to see it happen. You are special and you are here for a reason!

**How many lemons can you identify from this story and what are they?** Although we only focused on two lemons (suicidal ideations and depression), there were more. The tuition of $10,000 was a lemon, processing my mom's dating life was a lemon, and my dad's death was very much a lemon that was impacting me, even a year after his passing.

**How did the lemon(s) impact me?** All of the lemons made me depressed. I felt hopeless and helpless, and it felt like every time I took a step forward in the right direction, life kicked me back five steps. I was seriously ready to throw in the towel.

**Who was my pitcher (or the person I depended on)?** My pitcher was my siblings. Luckily they came home when they did and saved me. Although they didn't know what was going on in my life (and wouldn't find out until they were older), the fact that they came home early that day kept me from hurting myself and also gave me a new reason to live. They became my "why."

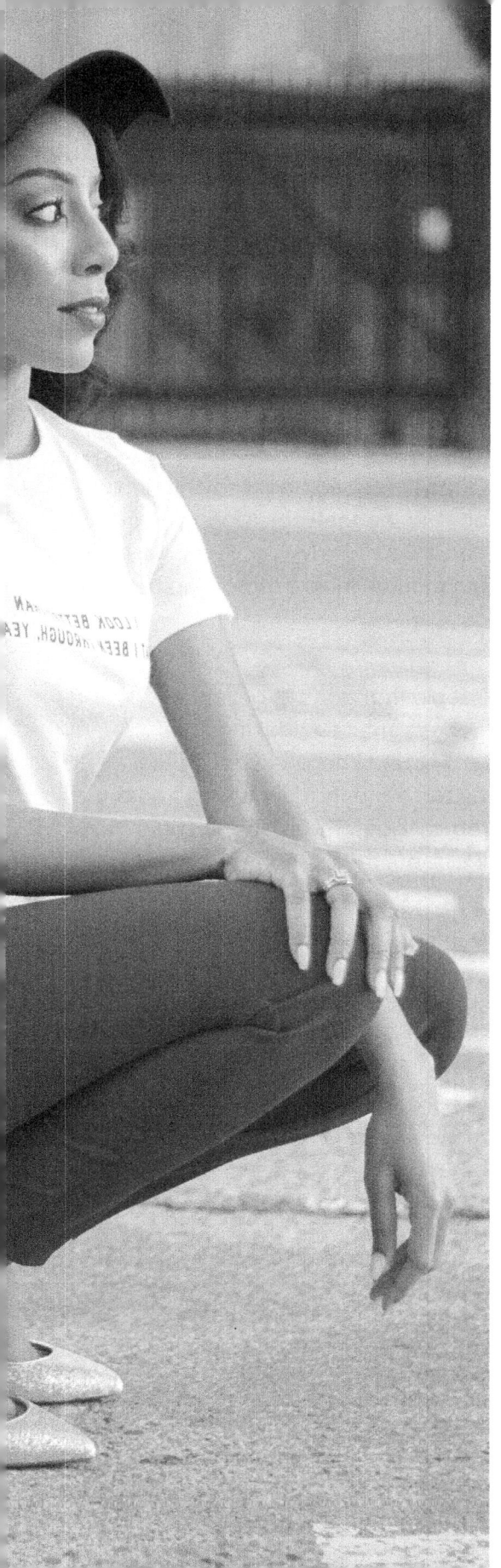

# Real Talk About Depression, Suicide, and Mental Illness

I never knew I struggled with depression until I became an adult and re-read my childhood journal entries. Based on my journal entries, my mood would shift every other day. Some days I was hopeful and felt as if I was on top of the world, and other days I was sad, lonely, and suicidal.

I remember having frequent fantasies about dying and no longer being on this earth, even when I was in elementary school. I think a lot of this was due to the fact that I was being abused and verbally assaulted, but didn't know how to process all of my emotions. I didn't share my emotions with anyone because I didn't know who to go to and I was scared. I kept so many of my emotions and feelings bottled up on the inside and the only way I felt in control was if I hurt myself.

**There are a few things I want you to remember about mental illness:**

# 1. There are many different types of mental illnesses.

**The best way to see if you are battling with mental illness is to seek professional help or schedule an appointment with your doctor for an evaluation; they can refer you to a specialist who can assist in diagnosing you.**

Considering all I've been through, I didn't start going to therapy until I was in graduate school at the age of 22. If I could go back in time, I would have done this a lot earlier in my life, but I didn't know better and didn't know this option existed for me.

Growing up in my household, we NEVER talked about therapy or mental illness. I was told to "pray the bad feelings away", that "therapy was for white people" and that my temperamental auntie was "just crazy."

Though many of us have heard similar statements and probably even laughed at them and used them as well, they're dangerous. These kinds of comments lead to stigma around getting help, but let me tell you, I'm one of the strongest people I know, and today I ask for all the help I need. I still go to therapy and I still struggle with depression to this day! There are good days and bad days.

# 2. You can't just turn the feelings you're having off.

Often times people will say "Just think positive thoughts" or "Don't you care about your family?" or "Get over it", but mental illness is something out of our control.

People that don't experience depression or suicidal thoughts really can't imagine what it's like for someone that deals with it on a regular basis. These people mean well… but they just don't get it.

Don't get me wrong, when I have low energy or go through a depressive state, I still think positive thoughts as I move through the feelings, but I can't control the sad and low moments. At this point in my journey, I've learned to move through them until I get to the other side.

If the other side doesn't come for you, it might be time to explore therapy, meeting with a psychiatrist or another mental health provider to see what your options are.

Don't shame yourself for having feelings that are outside of your control. You're doing the best you can with the mental state you're in.

## 3. You're not alone.

I get it. Sometimes the pain is so deep and the hurt is so present and it feels like you're the only one experiencing tough times and no one else understands. I've been there and even though I'm a motivational speaker and an inspiration for others, I still have these low moments to this day.

I was recently struggling with a health issue that could impact my ability to have children, and make me susceptible to diabetes. When I got the news, I was devastated. "Haven't I already been through enough?" I asked myself. After I gave myself time and space to cry, vent, and be angry, I got into what I like to call Creative Resiliency Mode.

This is the space I move into after I've processed bad news or an unfortunate situation. I get creative and think of ways to overcome the issue and seek out people who are struggling with what I'm struggling with. In this case, I went to YouTube

and started Googling the condition my doctor said I had, Polycystic Ovarian Syndrome (PCOS).

I found hundreds, if not thousands of women who were struggling with PCOS and thriving. This inspired me and helped me realize that I'm not alone. There are other people out there that have information I lack that could allow me to get the breakthrough I was seeking.

Wherever you are in your journey, try to seek out positive online communities of like-minded people, or create your own community for people like you.

Once I began to tell my story, I realized that there were more women who were suffering in silence that had PCOS as well. You are not alone.

## 4. There's no one size fits all solution for mental illness.

Although humans have a lot in common, we're also very different. What works for one person's situation may not work for another person. The best we can do is try and see what works for us.

When tough situations arise, tap into your Creative Resiliency Mode, do your Googles, see what other people have tried, and consult with positive people in your life to see what might work for you.

When I was a teen, I got on birth control to help with my acne. Years later, as I read my journal entries I realized that the birth control I was taking contributed to my depression, anxiety, and suicidal thoughts. Some of my friends took the same pill and they were fine.

Since then, I've decided to change my birth control method. I've also started going to therapy regularly and I've changed up my diet and became a pescatarian (for me this means I am a vegetarian that eats seafood and no dairy) which has helped my mental health tremendously. I don't get depressed often but when I do, I manage it based on what's worked for me in the past.

It's all about finding a solution that works for you, but in order to do that, you have to be here.

## 5. Your self-care is crucial and it must be maintained.

Everyone is talking about self-care these days. It's like a new wave or fad, but a good one indeed.

Self-care in a nutshell is any activity that we intentionally do in order to take care of our mental, emotional, and physical health. The thing about it is, self-care looks different for everyone. No matter your age or background, you can benefit from a regular self-care practice.

For me, self-care includes therapy, phone calls with my siblings, exercise, massages, manicures and pedicures, spa days, twerk classes with my girls, and meditating.

The same way we take showers or baths daily to cleanse our bodies, we should also practice self-care daily to cleanse our mental and emotional beings. Nothing in this world is "set it and forget it". Everything must be maintained.

## 6. Therapy is dope.

If you've never been to therapy, it's really dope if you find the right therapist. We need to think about a new therapist the same way we think about a new boo. You date them for a while and if they're a good fit, you take it to the next level.

Therapists are human beings; sometimes we click with them and other times we don't. I've had 4 official therapists in my life and while the first two were ehhh, only okay, my most recent therapists were bomb!

I'd see one of my therapists every Saturday and basically talked to her about the same stuff I'd tell my best friend. Talking to my therapist was often better because I could talk about me and only my problems for the whole hour and my therapist would guide me toward finding my own direction and healing. If that's not dope, then I don't know what is.

At one point, before I found a therapist in my new neighborhood, I was going through a really tough time. My family wasn't available, my best friend was pregnant and busy, and my husband was working, so I did something I NEVER thought I'd do... I called a suicide prevention hotline.

At first I felt so weird calling a random stranger to tell them about my problems, but I really didn't want to share my situation with anyone in my circle and I figured a stranger's help was better than suffering by myself.

Believe it or not, the call helped a lot! I cried on the phone and let out all the feelings I had. Although it didn't take all the pain away, I felt much better getting my emotions out of my system.

My cohost and I actually dedicated a podcast episode, So What's Therapy Like Anyway?, to those considering therapy for the first time. We share tips on what to ask your therapist and what to expect during the process.

## Resources for you from the National Institute of Mental Health:

**Step 1:** If you are not sure where to turn, you can use TXT 4 HELP Interactive (www.nationalsafeplace.org/txt-4-help), which allows you to text live with a mental health professional. You can also call the National Suicide Prevention hotline at 1-800-273-8255.

**Step 2:** "Make an appointment with your doctor for an evaluation. Your doctor can make sure you don't have a physical illness that may be affecting your mental health. Your doctor may also talk to you about the possibility of seeing a mental health professional, such as a psychiatrist, counselor, psychologist, or therapist. These practitioners can diagnose and treat depression and other mental disorders."

# Let's Chat!

## How do you feel after reading the last chapter?

Whew! Chapter 3 was a lot. If you've ever struggled with depression, suicidal ideations, or any other mental illness, that chapter may have been triggering for you.

Even if you've never struggled with any of those personally, if you care about or love someone that has, it may have been a tough chapter to read for you too. I just want to take a moment to acknowledge you and celebrate you because this can't be easy.

You're reading a book that's challenging (and supporting) you to dig deep into the ugly parts of life that many people don't talk about. Many people would rather pretend the past didn't happen and keep pushing because it's painful to face the truth, to face the emotions that the past brings forth.

The thing is, in order to truly heal and flourish, we must face what happened and figure out how we plan to move forward.

You are brave, you are courageous, and you are smart! Only a person with those attributes would read a book like this. Although chapter 3 may have been tough, I hope that you were also encouraged by the stories mentioned. There are so many people struggling but they still show up, they still make lemonade, they still inspire others... and you can do the same.

Let's take a moment and reflect on what you've read so far.

**How do you feel?**




**What's coming up for you?**




**What are you thinking about?**

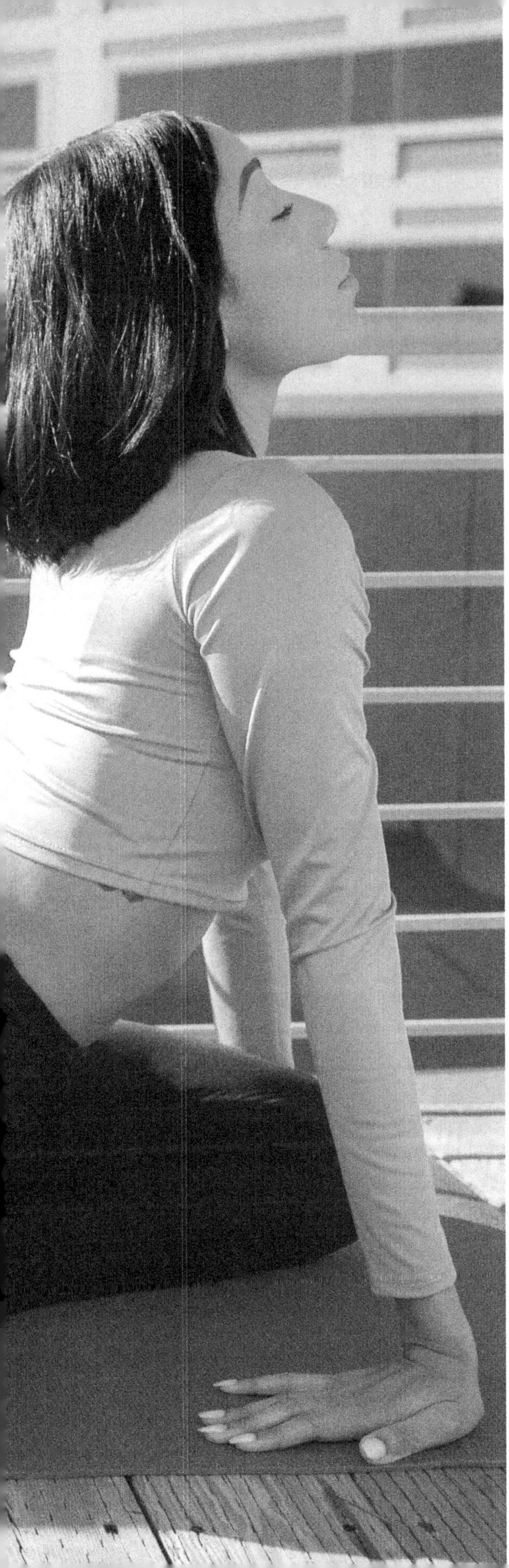

# Chapter 4
# The Sugar F.A.C.E

I'm lying on my bed in my first apartment with two pillows propping my head up, and my mind is racing as I gaze up at the ceiling and think to myself.

*OMG, I did it! I graduated from college, I moved to Maryland by myself, and now I'm in grad school. I have my own car, my own place, I'm making my own money, and I'm pursuing another degree. I'm literally doing all the things that I said I wanted to do when I was in high school.*

*The weird thing is, depression, anxiety, and low self-esteem followed me to Maryland.*

*How though? I moved far away from where all of the trauma happened, I had a better life and I was making it in the world but they still managed to travel with me and make a cozy place for themselves in my new life.*

## "The weird thing is, depression, anxiety, and low self-esteem followed me to Maryland."

I had just broken up with a crazy controlling boyfriend that tried to manipulate me and control every aspect of my life, so I was happily single and ready to find the real me.

I realized that for a long time prior to this move, I was never truly by myself. I've always had roommates, family around, a boyfriend distracting me, or I was busy just to be busy.

Having my own place forced me to be with myself and I couldn't escape me because no matter where I went, I was there. This is what I needed the most: me time.

## "Imagine getting to the top of the mountain just to find out it isn't as lit as they said it would be?"

As I began to sit with myself in silence, journal, reflect on my life, and get real with myself, I came to the realization that even though I made it this far, I still had tons of invisible symptoms from my childhood lingering within.

I was insecure, afraid to speak up in class, I felt like I was walking around as a fake person because I was afraid to show the world the real me... I honestly didn't really know who I was but I knew for sure I wasn't the person I was showing my coworkers and friends. I'd agree with things I didn't really understand or agree with. I'd pretend to be happy even though I wasn't. I just felt so uncomfortable being in my skin.

I read the self-help, feel-good books, I went to church and prayed, I read my Bible but I felt like I needed more. I did pretty much all I could do on my own and now I needed outside help.

Imagine getting to the top of the mountain just to find out it isn't as lit as they said it would be? What would you do?

# If you fail to plan, you plan to fail

It became clear to me that there was no place in the world I could go that

would make me happy. There was no partner or lover that I could find that could complete me. There was no goal or dream that would fulfill me the way I wanted to be fulfilled. I had to be my own source of happiness and wholeness.

So I created a plan. I've heard this quote before, "If you fail to plan, you plan to fail." It's like getting in your car with a GPS and not putting an address in, but deciding to drive around.

You'd literally end up in a random place because you don't have a specific location in mind. You'd drive around aimlessly being led by traffic, impacted by other people on the road that might know their destination, but you're kind of just driving along for the ride. It'd be pointless, right?

I also added some personal goals.

I wrote down that I planned to be confident, humble, secure, whole, successful, a best-selling author, compassionate, and a list of other adjectives and attributes that I wanted my future self to exhibit.

I dedicated my 2-year grad school journey to my professional and personal development. Who cares whether I have a story if I didn't come out better on the other side?

This new journey was all about turning bitterness to betterness so I could truly inspire others with my story of overcoming obstacles, but I also embraced the healing process for my own health and sanity.

# From Bitterness to Betterness

My plan or GPS, came in the form of a vision board, but not the typical cutesy boards you see on social media. My vision board came with an action plan because without action, those visions wouldn't come true.

I added my dream car and house, my future husband, and money goals, but

# So what's the sugar F.A.C.E.?

When making lemonade, sometimes you need to add sugar to make it taste better. Sugar represents your own personal development, the shifts in your perspective that'll allow you to see a bigger vision for your life, and the steps to heal yourself on the journey. The Sugar F.A.C.E empowers you to go from bitterness to betterness.

We all have a story, but it's hard to inspire other people and turn our pain into purpose if we're not flourishing. What makes my story "special" or inspiring is the fact that I'm okay today. I am better instead of bitter. I have hope to offer others. Some of the most important personal development ideas are represented with the acronym, F.A.C.E. F- forgive yourself, A- address conflict constructively, C- choose your own adventure from the end to the beginning, E- embrace a victor-hood mentality.

**We'll dive deeper into each of these ideas in the following pages.**

# The Sugar F.A.C.E - Forgive Yourself

Forgiveness is tough, especially when we're working on forgiving ourselves. If you're like me and tend to be hard on yourself, then you probably struggle with forgiving yourself for mistakes and bad decisions. I've had to forgive myself for a lot but there's one situation I really want to share with you!

## My Poisonous Prince Charming: Why I Stayed in a Controlling Relationship

A couple days ago, my bestie, Amina, and I were having some girl talk as I unpacked my new apartment. Our conversation shifted to relationships, and we both reminisced on the B.S. that we've put up with in the past; much of the B.S. coming in the form of a controlling relationship or two.

Just thinking about my past relationships made me a bit weepy as I was reminded of how low my self-esteem was, and how much time I wasted being in something that I knew would bear no fruit. I knew I'd never marry my ex, but I had a bad habit of letting guys pressure me into relationships.

After all, when you're in the process of rebuilding your self-esteem and re-inventing yourself, flattery and attention can go a long way.

## From Friends to Lovers

My ex and I (we'll call him Shane), met online. We were friends over the phone for two years and cultivated a great friendship. We talked about our previous relationships, school, work, our family, everything. We became best friends.

After two years of talking, we agreed that it was time to hang out in person. I mean, I talked to his mom, he talked to my mom, and he didn't seem like a crazy person over the course of those two years, so I decided to meet up with my "phone friend."

Long story short- when we met we both had butterflies, we heard the angels singing, and we swore it was love at first sight. Needless to say, we were boo'd up soon after meeting.

In the beginning, everything was great, as it usually is. He respected me, and I respected him. He supported my goals and aspirations, and I supported his. We appeared to be extremely compatible. It was perfect! If you were to ask me then, I'd tell you that I was madly in love!

## He Didn't Change, My Eyes Were Opened

Looking back, the red flags are clear as day, but I was oblivious at the time. For one, when Shane got upset, he was very disrespectful. He'd talk down to me, curse at me, and speak in such a way that made me feel inferior.

After a heated argument, he'd apologize incessantly and I'd forgive him. He was also very manipulative. Whenever he wanted his way or tried to justify his unreasonableness, he'd make excuses for himself and make me out to be the bad guy.

Oftentimes, I believed him. There were instances where he threatened to hurt himself or humiliate me if I didn't do what he said.

Shane was also very controlling and jealous. He demanded every minute of my time that wasn't occupied by school or work. There was no such thing as "me-time" when we dated. In his words, when I had "me-time," I was cheating on him with myself.

## Enough is Enough

Over the course of our relationship, I broke up with Shane several times. He'd treat me wrong. We'd argue. He'd cuss at me. I'd curse him out. He apologized. I let him back in. We continued this cycle until one day, I decided that I'd had enough. After a year of being in an emotionally draining and mentally abusive relationship, I mustered up the strength

and ended it.

The breaking point for me was when we attended a church banquet together. Shane and I were at a table with a few of my friends when the guy next to me (who happened to be like a little brother to me) asked me an innocent question. I forget what the question was, but it was super chill. I answered the guy's question and Shane flipped out!

He began texting my phone (right there at the banquet) stating that I was being disrespectful by talking to the guy next to me, as well as a bunch of other nonsense. After this incident, I knew I had to leave.

If I say I ended our relationship cold turkey, I'd be lying. I tried to wean us both off the relationship nice and slow. We tried the friend thing and even the friends with benefits thing, but it didn't work. We needed a serious break from each other, the relationship, and the toxicity.

## Why I Stayed in a Controlling Relationship

As much as I don't want to admit it, I was in love with Shane back then. The relationship began in a good place, and at one point, we made each other happy. When things went awry, I stayed for several reasons.

- [ ] **I stayed because he was my friend**
- [ ] **I thought he would change**
- [ ] **I invested so much in the relationship and I felt trapped**
- [ ] **I didn't want to hurt him**
- [ ] **I didn't want to be alone**
- [ ] **He was a good person with a bad temper**
- [ ] **I was so comfortable around him**
- [ ] **He met my family and I met his**
- [ ] **He knew me so well, and I didn't think anyone else would ever accept me like he did**
- [ ] **He was my first love**

I stayed in that relationship for so many reasons, but I left because I finally realized that the quality of my life had decreased while being in it. I finally realized that the reasons above were not good reasons at all. Some were valid points and experiences that I needed to accept and put behind me, while others were excuses I believed out of fear.

Just because you've been in something or in a certain place for a long time doesn't mean you have to stay if it's no longer good for you. It's never too late to start over or change your mind, no matter how impossible it seems today.

At first, I beat myself up for putting

up with such a relationship. I was disappointed in myself for wasting so much of my time on a relationship that didn't seem to be going anywhere. I felt dumb because I kept going back to someone who clearly didn't know how to treat me. I alienated myself from the people who loved me the most. I cut friends off who cared about me. I missed out on great friendships and new experiences- all because I wanted to please and appease him. I made a lot of bad decisions while I dated Shane, and it took me a long time to forgive myself and heal from the experience.

relationship with Shane. I wasn't as strong or as confident as I am today. If I was, Shane probably wouldn't even have wanted me because he would not have been able to use his manipulation and control over me.

That relationship taught me so much and gave me more compassion for other people that deal with and stay in toxic relationships. It's very hard to leave but I did- and that's something to be proud of. I also promised myself to always speak up for myself in future relationships, and cut someone off as soon as they continue to treat me with disrespect.

# We Deserve Forgiveness, Even From Ourselves

You deserve forgiveness for your mistakes, no matter how painful the consequences, for three reasons:

## 1) You made the only decision you could make, given your needs and awareness at that moment.

Based on where my self-esteem was, how mature I was, and what I knew, I did the best I could in my

## 2) You've already paid for your mistake. Your error led to painful consequences.

Most of us wouldn't kick someone if they're down, so we shouldn't do that to ourselves. Oftentimes when we make mistakes, there's a consequence we have to pay. If you're trying to deal and cope with the consequences in addition to shame, guilt, and unforgiveness, that's going to make it even harder to bounce back.

Usually when I eff up, I acknowledge it within myself, step back and see the situation for what it is. For instance, a

few years ago I was driving through a parking lot and hit another car. I know, I know. You'd have to be there to understand how it happened though. I swear the woman came out of nowhere and I t-boned her car.

To make matters worse, there was a child in the backseat! Luckily everyone was okay, but I was so embarrassed, stressed, and disappointed in myself. I'm a good driver, how did this happen? After I parked my car and took a breather, I looked at the facts: I hit her car, I made a mistake, everyone is okay, and I have insurance which will cover any damage.

Beating myself up anymore wouldn't help the situation. I had to let that go. Now, let's say that someone was hurt or seriously injured. In that case, I may have had to go to therapy to help me work through it because that's a heavy burden to carry. The most important thing to remember is, you never have to go at it alone. Whether you choose to call a hotline or go to therapy, it's a safe space and it's confidential.

## 3) Mistakes are unavoidable. You come into this world knowing nothing.

Everything you have learned, from standing upright to using a computer has been accomplished at the price of thousands of mistakes. It makes no sense to kick yourself for something you can only avoid in the cemetery.

We're all going to make mistakes for the rest of our lives. The goal is to get better each time and do our best to refrain from making the same mistakes over and over again. When we find ourselves revisiting the same mistakes, it might be time to seek help outside of ourselves - and that's perfectly okay.

## The Sugar F.A.C.E - Address Conflict in a Constructive Way

As you embark on your journey to self-healing and making lemonade, you may make some people angry. Some people won't understand why you're

bringing up the past and sharing your truth.

Some people will shame you for sharing your story and encourage you to keep quiet so you don't expose the dark things swimming under the surface. I say all that to say that on my journey to owning my truth and sharing my story, I've faced my share of conflict and difficult conversations. I want to share some tips with you that you can use on your journey.

In the story below, I'm going to take you back to a few years ago, right before I got married. I'm going to share with you one of the moments I had to remind my family members that I'm an adult while standing firm in my truth and clinging to my decisions. You may not be able to relate to this exact experience- and that's fine. I want you to think about the story and the lessons I share to see how you might use them in your own life.

## How to Walk Confidently In Your Independence, When Your Family Still Thinks You're a Kid

The past two years have brought about monumental life changes for me. But to my surprise, these great life changes were followed by challenging experiences that I thought would break me!

My husband always jokingly says that my family thinks I'm baby Jesus.

They are extremely proud of me, and they let me and everyone else know any chance they get.

I'm very close to my family and although I'm not the baby, I'm treated as such. It's probably because I'm my parents' first-born and everyone sort of watched me grow up.

The constant reminders about how I used to sleep on my uncle's chest as an infant, or how I used to run up on the pulpit at church with my grandfather when I was a toddler never gets old... and I get it.

I didn't always get it, but watching my siblings (aka my babies) grow up has given me a glimpse of what my parents, grandparents, and close family members see when they watch me flourishing into a woman.

## The Engagement

It all started when I got engaged in 2013. I made the announcement on Facebook and a few of my family members had some disapproving and unnecessary comments and left them on my page. The crazy part is the important people in my family like my

dad, mom, and grandparents met my fiancé and were totally supportive of us getting married.

6 months after I got engaged, I decided to move in with my fiancé. I initially didn't share this with my family because I just knew that I'd be judged and get unsolicited comments and I didn't feel as though I needed their approval. I come from a very religious family and... you know how that goes.

Oftentimes when we get into relationships, our family might be overprotective. Sometimes it's for a good reason like if you've ever dated a Shane, and other times it's because that's just what family does.

The thing about my fiancé is that he's a really good guy. He supports me wholeheartedly, pushes me to grow, respects me and his mom, and treats me like a Queen. I knew the relationship was the right one for me, regardless of what those family members said.

## The Wedding Date

In the fall of 2014, when I told my family that my fiancé and I had chosen our wedding date, all hell broke loose. The two people that I counted on to be in my corner... weren't.

To make a long story short, my mom was still in jail at the time and most likely wouldn't be released in time for the wedding. Being the respectful daughter that I am... I wrote her a heartfelt letter explaining to her that I didn't intend on putting my life on hold and waiting until she was released to get married.

No one had any idea when she'd be home and my fiancé and I started mapping out our future. In addition, I really wanted to get married on July 21st since it's Daddy's Death Anniversary.

Repurposing that day meant the world to me.

## The Drama

Needless to say, my mom didn't receive my message well. She called my grandmother, and they were both extremely hurt and disappointed with my decision.

They felt as though I should have waited until my mom got home to get married. I remember second-guessing myself, wondering if I should change the date.

My mom didn't call me for months while my grandmother wouldn't answer my phone calls. I was so hurt and felt alone.

At a time when my loved ones were supposed to be celebrating with me, they shunned me.

After a month or so, I finally spoke to my grandmother and had a heart to heart. I stood up to my mom and had one of those "I'm grown" talks when I was 18, but I never really needed to have one with my grandmother until now.

## The Talk

The talk was awkward, tense, and real but so necessary. Through tears, I told my grandmother how her actions made me feel, and I explained some of the points that I'm going to share with you below.

My mom and I finally spoke and a few months after my wedding date announcement, everyone started to come around. It was a long, depressing process but I'm so glad that I was steadfast in my resolve to have my wedding day on July 21, 2015.

Ultimately, my family understood where I was coming from, but it took me having difficult conversations and reminding them of a few things before they got to that point.

Sometimes it's necessary to stand alone in your independence in order for your family to respect you and your decisions.

## 1. People will only treat you the way that you demand to be treated

Now don't get it twisted- I have the utmost respect for my parents, grandparents and the elders in my family. However, I do believe that as we grow older, there's a certain level of mutual respect that should be reciprocated.

I am also in no way, shape, or form encouraging you to be disrespectful and go off on an "I'm grown, I can do what I want" rant to your family members. These experiences I'm sharing were at points in my life where I was out of the house, paying my own bills, and actively pushing toward my goals.

Okay, now that we've got that out of the way, let's get back on track.

My grandfather used to call the girls in the family "ugly" as a little joke. I hated it but didn't know how to approach him about it. Seeing as I struggled with low self-esteem and considering the reverence that I have for words, their power, and their impact on my life... I had to pull him aside and ask him to stop. I'll tell you more about the tools I

used to have this conversation in a bit.

I'm not confrontational and I'd much rather avoid conflict, but in order for me to walk into my independence confidently, I had to become comfortable having difficult conversations with the people that I love.

## 2. Go With Your Gut and Stick to Your Guns

Whether you're deciding on a new career path, going to an out-of-state school or gearing up for a relocation, trust yourself and be steadfast in your decision. If you change your mind that's okay, but be sure to be true to yourself.

Sometimes you have to stick to your guns in order to gain their respect. When I say go with your gut and stick to your guns, I'm referring to sound and well-thought-out plans and ideas for your life.

This isn't a cosign for the "we in love, and I'm going to go off to Vegas to marry my boo thang", let's be real here, k?

Another thing to be aware of is the fact that sometimes family members won't agree with your choices and may disown you, talk about you, or judge you for your decisions. If this is the case, you'll need to build up your support system (your pitcher) to help get you through the difficult times if you believe the decision you're making is worth the journey.

## 3. Humble Yourself and Pick up the Pieces

On your journey to walking in your independence, there will be times when you make mistakes and that's okay. Just be sure to humble yourself, take responsibility and move forward gracefully.

When I was with Shane, I cut off a lot of people for no reason and burned many bridges. As you can imagine, my family was very vocal about their opinion on my relationship and my boyfriend at the time.

In this situation, I actually knew that dude wasn't good for me, but I wanted to prove to my family that I could make decisions on my own, and I wanted to force them to respect me and my relationship.

I was dead wrong. I messed up important relationships trying to prove myself. Once I finally broke up with oh boy (Shane), I had to pick up the pieces that I had scattered behind me. I chose to apologize to my friends,

rekindle relationships, and fix what I had broken.

The craziness that this relationship brought into my life is now a running joke between my friends and me.

Remember- mistakes can be stepping stones in your journey. They don't define you.

# Why Does This Even Matter?

I'm going to share something with you that I learned later in life and wish I had known a lot sooner. The reason it's important to know how to resolve conflicts (and communicate) effectively is that everything you want in life is connected to a person. If we burn bridges, create drama within relationships, or get a bad reputation for causing trouble or being rude, word will get around and this could hold you back.

Think about it this way- the prayers you ask God for will come in the form of another human being. When you pray for a new job, God won't be walking down from Heaven to hire you; he's going to open a door of opportunity through a person. Not religious? I get it, stay with me for a sec though.

The dream job you plan to have one day will require you to work with people in some capacity- and the better your relationships with those people, the better chance you have of growing and working your way up in the company. Basically, your network determines your net worth. The people you know, and the people who know you and have good things to say about you will impact how much money you make and how far you go.

People also go above and beyond for people they like. By no means am I recommending being fake or not being true to yourself. What I'm saying is, if you can learn how to navigate conflict in a constructive way and state how you feel in a tactful manner, you'll go very, very far, my friend. Ask me how I know- I do this every day!

I've been developing my conflict resolution and communication skills for years, and I've been able to persuade a professor to turn a B to an A (because I was a good student and I was just a few points away from an A). I've also pulled one of my coworkers aside and confronted him about something he said about me by using a sandwich compliment (more on this later). He actually thanked me after the conversation and we have a great friendship today. It's not necessarily what you say, but how you say it.

# Tips for resolving conflicts and having difficult talks

## Tip #1: Cool off

Most times when we take action while we're heated, we end up regretting something about our behavior. Before you address the conflict, give yourself time and space to cool down so you can truly say what you mean and mean what you say when the time comes.

Remember, your main goal (outside of resolving the conflict) is to make sure the other person understands where you're coming from. Breathe deeply while making a calming statement like, "I am calm, cool, and collected." Look at the sky, clear your desk or straighten up, splash cold water on your face, write in a journal, or take a quick walk before coming back to talk about the problem.

Some people need physical release, while others need something quiet that engages their brain like a puzzle, book, or word game. Determine what works for you and use it the next time you get angry. Then you'll be ready to go on to the next step.

## Tip #2: Express Yourself Using I-Statements

First, what is your main goal when expressing how you feel to the person you're in conflict with? I'd say that my main goals are to 1) get the other person to see things from my point of view, 2) take responsibility and apologize, and 3) make sure it doesn't happen again or come to a resolution.

I-statements are a sharp contrast to "you messages" which puts others on the defensive and closes the door to communication. A statement like, "You left the kitchen a mess again! Can't you ever clean up after yourself?" will escalate the conflict. Now take a look at how differently an I-statement comes across: "I'm annoyed because I thought we agreed we'd clean up the kitchen after using it. What happened?"

When making I-statements, it's important to avoid put-downs, guilt-trips, sarcasm, or negative body language. We need to come from a place inside us that's non-combative and willing to compromise. A key belief in conflict resolution is, "It's us against the problem, not us against each other." I-statements allow us to convey this.

## Tip #3: Use Reflective Listening

Reflective listening is you mirroring what the person just said so you can make sure 1) to let them know you heard them, and 2) you understood what they said.

Reflective listening requires you to really listen to the person and not try to think of your response as they're talking.

When you want to let someone know that you're not just listening to them but actually hearing them, you can use some of these suggested phrases below. You can also use a combination of them, depending on the situation.

## Tip # 4: Use the sandwich compliment

Whenever I have to "tell someone about themselves" but want to make sure they actually receive the message, I use my favorite tool in my conflict resolution toolkit- the sandwich compliment.

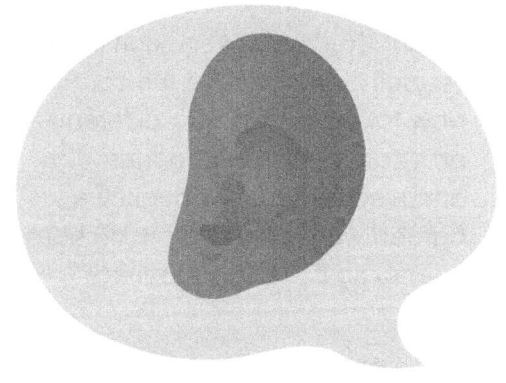

*"Oh, okay."*

*"That makes sense."*

*"Gotcha."*

*"Sounds good."*

*"I feel you."*

**Here's how it works:**

The first piece of bread on the sandwich represents your introduction to what you actually want to say. This should be a compliment or disarming statement. The purpose of the compliment is to open the person up and make sure they'll be receptive to what you have to say. If you begin with your real concern, they'll likely be defensive right away.

The middle of the sandwich or the meat of the conversation will be your concern or what you want to bring to their attention.

Lastly, you'll close out with another genuine compliment or something positive to leave a good taste in their mouth, and ensure that you can have positive interactions moving forward.

Take a look at the example below. The scenario is, two good friends, Toya and Christina, had a conflict and Toya wants to share her concern with Christina. Watch how Toya uses the sandwich compliment along with some of the other tips above.

*First piece of bread*

"Christina, when I first came to this school, you were one of my first best friends. You showed me around and made me feel like I belong and that was really dope."

*The last piece of bread:*

"We got so close this past year, and I really hope we can move past all this drama."

*The meat*

"I was hurt, honestly, I was big mad when you told Sam and Jenna that I had to borrow a pad from you in gym class. I didn't understand why my personal business was shared with them. What happened?"

# The Sugar F.A.C.E- Choose Your Own Adventure From End to Beginning

## Things Might Start Off Rough

I remember it like it was yesterday, my bus driver Mr. Bob just picked up my little sister and I from school, and drops us off at "home." Home is a place I'd never invite my friends to. Home is a place I'm embarrassed by. Home is a place I pretend I don't live. Home is a one-bedroom shelter that houses my mom, Daddy, 4 younger siblings and I. We're living in Chester, Pennsylvania; a city with a lot of talent… but a pretty bad reputation.

I've been through a lot, but this is one of the most stressful, depressing, and embarrassing circumstances my family has experienced. We've been homeless before, but this was different.

When I was younger and we lived in California, we lived in motels or crashed with family and friends- but back then, we were only a family of 5. I was also younger, so I didn't understand the magnitude of our predicament. This time, there are 7 of us and I'm in high school, so I have a better understanding of just how bad it is.

I'm constantly depressed but I'm a great actress, so despite how bad my home life is, I'm all smiles when I get to school. My deceptive smile hides the pain so my friends don't ask questions, allowing me to fit in with everyone else and mask the shame and discomfort. Do you know what it's like to hide behind a fake smile?

When I get "home", my routine is to eat a snack, take a bath to relax, and climb up to the top bunk in the bedroom my 4 siblings and I share; I journal with music blasting from my headphones. I cry myself to sleep most nights because I'm sad. *Why me? Why does my family always have to struggle?* I feel so hopeless and helpless.

## Depend on Your Pitcher When You Need Help

My family is relatively religious, and although church used to be super boring when I was younger, our new church is pretty cool. My pastor, Pastor Collins, is hip and his messages really hit home. I feel like I can actually relate to his sermons, and to be honest, they give me life. The church is also extremely helpful to my family.

During the Christmas season, my pastor's family helps my parents get gifts for me and my siblings. They host food drives so we could have more food options, but to be frank, the most useful gift for me are the sermons and motivation.

Pastor Collins always says, "If you can see it in your mind, you can see it in real life." He also says that "If you can get the spirit of the thing, you can get the thing." This spoke to me because even though my situation wasn't ideal, his message gave me hope for a better tomorrow.

I figured if I began to close my eyes and think about my future and everything I actually wanted, despite what my current situation was, maybe I could actually get it. I began signing my journal entries as, "Future bestselling author, Terri Lomax"

" Future businesswoman" and "Future millionaire."

Pastor Collins inspired me to dream big and realize that I don't have to be confined to the dreams of my family members or their limitations. I don't have to believe what statistics say about "at-risk" teens like me because I can dare to dream big. I'm allowed to want more for my life and achieve my wildest dreams, even if no one in my family has embarked on that journey. And guess what? You can too!

## No Matter How You Got Here, You're Here for a Reason

A few years ago, my mom and I were having girl talk and she told me a story that almost left me speechless.

When my mom got pregnant with me she was abroad in Japan as a sailor in the Navy at only 19 years old. My mom was devastated when she found out she was pregnant! She wasn't married and was so young. She didn't know what to do.

She considered having an abortion at first. She visited one doctor and tried to schedule the abortion, but for some reason, she wasn't able to do it; the doctor wouldn't let her. She went to a different doctor and again, the doctor advised her not to do it for some

reason. She tried one final doctor's visit with another doctor and that doctor also wouldn't go through with the abortion. My mom was so confused but figured this was a sign to keep her baby.

When she finally mustered up the courage, she called my grandparents and they were actually more supportive than she expected.

This story blew me away. As my mom and I sat there crying and talking, she said, "Now I know why I wasn't able to go through with the abortion, and I'm so glad I didn't. You were supposed to be here."

## But Wait, There's More...

Fast forward a few years after this conversation, and I'm all grown up, living in San Francisco with my husband. The dreams I wrote down in my journal are finally coming true. I'm a national motivational speaker, I have a successful podcast with a global reach, a book, and I'm making a name for myself in the tech industry.

As I continue to evolve, I get curious about my past, my ancestors, and where my family came from. I sign up for an Ancestry.com account, and my husband and I send in our DNA so we can build out our family tree before we have kids.

On September 15th, I wake up and attempt to give myself a pep talk so I can get out of bed and get ready for work, but I see a notification from Ancestry.com; my results are finally in! I'm ecstatic.

I finally get to find out where my family is from in Africa and what my estimated ethnic makeup includes. When I open the app and review my results, I immediately go into shock.

In addition to finding my African ancestry, the app connects me with a man I've never seen in my life but who has a familiar face. Ancestry.com tells me that this man, whose screen name is something like Navy4Life11, is my biological father!

I immediately text my best friend a picture of the man and ask her, " Hey Mina, do me and this guy look alike?" She responds with an enthusiastic, "Yes! OMG, is that your uncle?" I'm literally frozen. WTF is all I can think.

I call my mom to share the news, and she's just as confused as I am. After a few days of researching, my mom reflecting on her time in the Navy, and me asking Ancestry for a new DNA kit, we finally get to the bottom of this and figure out what happened. You won't believe it, because I still can't!

My mom and the only biological father I've ever known, took a break in the Navy and as you can imagine, teenagers in Japan are probably having lots of fun. Long story short, Navy4Life11 and my mom got a little close and boom, I was conceived. I know, crazy right? I'll have to tell you more about this story in another book or on my podcast.

## Trust Me on This One

To some people, I'd be considered an "accident" or an "oops baby", but guess what? Your parents are simply the vehicles that ushered you into this world so you could fulfill your purpose. Regardless of how you got here, you were the one who made it- and you made it for a reason.

Sometimes it takes a long while for us to figure out why we're here. There's a quote by Mark Twain that says, "The two most important days in your life are the day you are born, and the day you find out why." The thing is, you have to live life long enough and continue to dream big enough to find the why that makes it all come full circle. Sometimes the biggest challenge is seeing life past your circumstances and seeing the light even when you're in the dark tunnel.

# The secret to seeing it before you see it

What we think and say about ourselves leads to what we see and believe about ourselves. Our words and thoughts have more power than we realize.

I've had a diary for as long as I can remember. During one of the darkest phases of my life (which happened to be high school), I journaled nearly every day. To date, I have about 6 or 7 composition books filled with my experiences and life lessons from over the years.

Every once in a while, I reread my journal entries. It blows me away when I see myself writing my dreams into existence. I talk about future happiness, my motivational speaking career, being financially independent and being confident. I was a broke teenager in a very bad space in life living in a shelter, but I wrote about my future as if I was the author of my own story. I wrote about being happy even though I was sad. I didn't let my predicament dictate my vision. I learned that life is like a choose-your-own adventure game. I spoke exactly what I wanted as if I had the power to choose. I later found out that I do have that power - and you do too, even if you don't believe it yet.

If you're thinking that you're too young or too old to do something great in the world or pursue your dreams... yea right! Remember those lemons you read about in the earlier activity? Many of them are from people that society might say are too young to make a difference. And then you have people like, Vera Wang, who entered the fashion industry when she was 40 years old. Samuel L. Jackson finally got a starring role in Spike Lee's movie, *Jungle Fever* when he was 46 years old. And of course there's Representative Maxine Waters, who fearlessly represents California's 43rd congressional district at 81. The list goes on and on. There are no excuses, my friend!

## Your Dream is Bigger Than Your Obstacles

Write your vision out and visit it daily. I'm a living witness that if you continue

to meditate on your vision and you take the steps necessary to make your vision a reality, it will happen. The secret for me was persistence. I'm still waiting for some of my other visions to come past, but I truly believe they'll manifest one day.

When I was younger, my pastor used to say, "You have to see a thing in your mind before you can see it in your reality." Before we dive into the next activity, let's work on shifting our perspective and enter the world of limitless possibilities. I dare you to dream big, just like I did.

**In the glasses below, write down some of the goals you plan to achieve in your life. Be specific and remember there are no limitations. Close your eyes when you're finished, and actually imagine yourself doing what you wrote down. If that tiny voice in your head says it's too big or impossible, that means you're on the right track - write it down anyway!**

# A Goal Map to Your Dreams

Failing to have a dream is like getting into your car without putting an address into the GPS, but hoping to get somewhere cool. Without direction, action steps, or milestones, you'll drive around aimlessly, most likely taking unnecessary detours, and getting stuck in traffic with some people that may know where they're going and others who are just as lost as you are.

Many people talk about the great things they want to accomplish, and often fantasize about their dreams because that's the easy part. It doesn't require a plan, action, or accountability.

The real ones, the ones that get stuff done and actually make progress, they're the ones that create a goal map- a plan for actually getting to the end goal. These are the people that put an address in the GPS, start the engine, and drive off.

## But What if You Don't Know What You Want?

Guess what? When I was in high school, I didn't really know what I wanted to be when I grew up. Even in college, I had an idea, but I didn't know for sure. My career choices changed as much as the weather. At first, I wanted to be a fashion designer, then a psychologist, then a career counselor. Then I stopped thinking about what I wanted to be and thought about the lifestyle I wanted to live.

I knew what I wanted to be able to do for sure. I wanted to travel, I wanted financial security so my future family would never be homeless, I wanted to have a nice car, money in the bank, and I wanted to make a positive impact on the world. I know you're probably thinking, "Well, Terri, knowing what kind of lifestyle I want won't help me choose a career path or find my purpose." Just follow me for a minute.

The other thing I knew for sure was what I didn't want. Sometimes getting clear on what you don't want will lead you closer to what you want. I knew I didn't want to be broke. I didn't want to struggle. I didn't want to be involved in criminal activity. I didn't want to be in a toxic relationship. I didn't want to have kids at a young age.

With all of these things in mind, I began to map out a plan. I also went online to research various careers, and learn more about how much money I needed to make to have the lifestyle I desired. The plan changed a lot,

but who cares if the plan changes as long as you have a plan? Without a plan for yourself, you'll get sucked into someone else's plan for you, so it's best to start with a rough plan and tweak it along the way. I would revisit my plan on a weekly basis, check in with myself to see what changed and alter my direction if needed.

It's like being in the car with your GPS, but deciding to go down a new path so you can be rerouted. You won't have all the answers mapped out; I didn't either but I had something to work with. I also worked backwards, which I believe is the best way to map out your goals. Think of the end goal, and determine what steps will lead you to the desired outcome.

Take a look at the guide below to see how I reversed-engineered the way to my end goals. Be sure to pay close attention, because you'll be doing this for yourself afterwards.

## How to Goal Map Like a Boss

1. Write down a specific, measurable and realistic goal. Just to be sure we're on the same page, I've given you an example. A general goal would be, "I want to save more money." A specific goal would be "I want to save $1200 by the end of the year." To make sure your goal is measurable, think about how you'll know once you've accomplished the goal. In addition, a realistic goal can be grand, however it should be within reach, and achievable with hard work and dedication. The more detailed you are, the better chance you have of achieving your goal.
2. Write down the next step you'd need to take to achieve the goal, then the next step, and the step after that. Keep going until it leads you to your end result. For instance, if you want to save $1200 by the end of the year, this means you'll want to look at your paycheck and decide how much money you can afford to save each month, then each week. Your next step might be to save $100 a month. The step after that might be to put aside $25 every week once you get paid. The final step to help you get to the end goal could be to set up an automatic withdrawal for $25 every Friday from your bank account into a savings account so you don't forget to save. There you have it!
3. What isn't examined can't be improved, so you'll want to check in with yourself either every week or every 2 weeks. During these check-ins, you'll

want to review your big goal and ask yourself if it's still something you want to pursue. If it isn't, repeat steps 1 and 2. If the goal remained the same, see how you're progressing and figure out what you can do better. Keep this process going for each of your goals, and you'll be on your way to achieving your wildest dreams.

## Choose Your Own Adventure Goal Mapping Plan

**Start Here**

**Congratulations! You did it!**

## Directions

Use the space below to write down 3 big goals. Remember to use the tips from the previous page to ensure your goal is clear, specific, and measurable. Underneath each goal, write down the next steps you need to take to get you to the end goal. Next, add your 3 big goals near the target on the map, and write down the action items you'll need to complete for goals 1-3 on the map in the order in which you need to complete them.

| **Goal 1** | **Goal 2** | **Goal 3** |
|---|---|---|
| **Step 1** | **Step 1** | **Step 1** |
| | | |
| **Step 2** | **Step 2** | **Step 2** |
| | | |
| **Step 3** | **Step 3** | **Step 3** |
| | | |
| **Step 4** | **Step 4** | **Step 4** |

# A Letter to You, From You

Visualization has been a powerful vehicle in my journey from the bottom. One activity that provides a lot of healing, hope, clarity, and closure is writing a letter to your younger self or present self, from your future self. Here's how it works:

Close your eyes and picture yourself all glow'd up, whatever that means to you. You are successful, happy, and living your best life.

The stressors in your life right now have been alleviated. Any pain you're facing right now has subsided and life is absolutely amazing.

Sit with that for a minute and think about how it feels. Think about how much you've been through, and how much you've accomplished in your life.

Now I want you (your future self) to sit down, get comfy and write a letter encouraging your younger self. Your future self knows how the story turns out, so what will you tell your younger self about the you right now?

This is unique to you, but once you get started, the words will probably flow. Write whatever you need to. Address any issues you had in your life and give yourself some love. Forgive yourself, forgive others, be empathetic, and write until you feel you've addressed everything and provided your younger self with the hope you might need.

Explain to your younger self what is about to happen, and how they should react. Be loving, kind, and supportive at all times. Reassure your younger self.

**If you need an example to get your creative juices flowing, read my letter to my younger self below and either use it as a guide, or start from scratch and create your own structure. After you write your letter, I want you to read it often for inspiration. Years from now, you'll be able to revisit the letter- like I do with my journal entries- and you'll see just how far you've come.**

# Babygirl,

I know life is really hard right now and you feel like giving up. I really wish I could take your pain away so you wouldn't have to deal with it. I know it's hard being 17 and all you want to do is get away from mommy, daddy, and the kids, but please spend more time with them.

I'm sorry to break it to you... but you only have a few more months with daddy. As much as he annoys you, you'd give anything to see him again and hear those corny jokes and see his old school dance moves.

College is going to be one of the best and most challenging experiences for you, and you're going to have a moment when you want to give up and throw in the towel but please don't give up. A few years after graduating you're actually going to be that author and motivational speaker you've always written about in our diary. You won't quite be a millionaire, but you'll be earning 6 figures by yourself before you reach 30.

Babygirl, all the pain you've experienced in life is going to help hundreds, if not thousands of other people push through their pain to get to purpose and healing. Please keep pushing. Your future success will make all those nights you cried yourself to sleep worth it.

## <3 Future Terri

# Your Letter to Your Younger Self

**Follow the instructions on the previous page and write a letter to your younger self in the space provided below.**

# The Sugar F.A.C.E - Embrace a Victorhood Mentality

In September of last year, my husband and I prepped for the week which is our Sunday evening ritual. He took some Nyquil and slept upstairs in our bedroom; I chose to sleep on the couch because I ain't got time to be getting sick.

I'm on the couch sleeping with just a T-shirt on when something wakes me up around 2:30 AM. I look around and notice that the hallway light is on and there are slippers by the door.

I'm confused, but something doesn't feel right. I go upstairs, wake my husband up and ask him if he left the house (since he was on call, this was very likely).

He woke up a bit groggy and was completely lost when I asked him if he'd left the house. He said no, so I told him about the slippers and the light in the hallway. We both walked downstairs and looked around and you will not believe what we found in our home office...

A woman sleeping on the floor! The woman was curled up in the fetal position with her belongings around her... in my home office! The same office I blog in, the same office that holds all my equipment, my personal family files- I mean everything. What the entire *&%$?

As you can imagine, so many things crossed my mind. Long story short, my husband woke the woman up and she was clearly on something. She asked if she could just stay there until the morning (ummm no), but she refused to leave, so I called the cops. I also started recording because she was white and we're black... we know how this stuff goes. The cops came and identified her as a homeless woman from the area. We have no idea how she got into our apartment, but we're assuming the door must not have closed all the way at the end of the night.

We inspected the house later and noticed that the woman got some juice from our fridge — which is right

next to the knives in the kitchen, and the couch I was sleeping on. Traumatizing isn't even the word. I didn't sleep for days!

## The Aftermath

I went to work the next day and I was shook. Luckily, I was participating in this program called the Conscious Leadership Group (CLG), which really helped me process this incident.

I probably told this story over 50 times at this point. I spoke to my friends, my family, my colleagues - anyone who would listen.

I was scared, I was traumatized, and I wanted others to know what happened to me and offer some hope. This ish was crazy!

I had a chance to speak to the facilitator from CLG who totally blew me away. I told her about what happened, and after validating my feelings, she asked me a few questions:

Are you safe now? (Me: Yes.)

Are you in danger now? (Me: No.)

Will you do anything differently to prevent this from happening? (Me: Of course! I'm going to lock my top lock every night.)

Then she basically told me that I was re-victimizing myself by staying in that state of fear and distress, replaying the story, retelling the story, and pondering on the "what ifs."

I was blown because part of me felt like she was minimizing what happened to me... but then I thought about how I moved on from trauma in the past- and she was right.

## Heart to Heart Reflection

This whole victimhood vs victorhood mentality shift can be tricky. Many of us were actually victimized. We may have been hurt, betrayed, abused, or abandoned, which technically makes us a victim. But when you think about it, we have the choice to either wear that victim badge, hold on to what happened, and stunt our victim badge like it's a new accessory... or we can muster up the strength and refuse to let those experiences define us by letting go and redefining who we are.

### "Yes, we may have been victimized but let's refuse to let that be the end of the story."

What happened to us does not define us. We have the power to determine who we will become and how we will

show up in life. Playing the victim role is easy and has many benefits, doesn't it? You get attention, sympathy, it lets you off the hook, and some people may even take it easy on you, but it robs us of living in our true power. It may not feel like it inside, but you have the power within you to overcome what you're facing. It's all about your mindset and how you choose to show up in life.

The people that adopt the victim mentality usually don't lead happy lives. They have trouble in their relationships- can you guess why? Because they are always playing the victim role and see the world as though everything is happening to them. No one likes to be around someone that has given their power away and doesn't take responsibility for anything, you know?

Can you imagine where I'd be if I looked at my circumstances, and embraced what society and statistics say about people who come from where I come from? Imagine if I said, "Well, all this bad stuff happened in my life, so I guess I have an excuse to be an alcoholic, a drug addict, a prison inmate, or living in poverty." Playing the victim role is like quitting the game before you even get on the court.

I have a few questions for you that I want you to reflect on below. We're going to have a heart to heart. No judgment, just honesty with yourself.

**What are you holding onto that's causing you to see yourself as a victim?**

**When you hit a setback or fail at something how do you process it? Do you blame others, or do you take responsibility and commit to doing your best in the future?**

**Share any other thoughts...**

## How to Go From Victim to Victor

Even though I was physically and verbally abused as a child, grew up poor, and faced a great deal of adversity in my life, I have the power to choose the narrative that I tell myself. I have the choice to grow to the victor stage. When we hang out in victim-land, we replay the events that happened to us and keep telling the same story about how we were violated or traumatized- sometimes we even relive it in our body.

You know what's wild? When we keep replaying those events that happened we are literally re-traumatizing our body; our mind and body doesn't know the difference between the real thing and the replay we highlight in our mind. The same energies and endorphins are released for both!

That's what I did when we had the home intruder situation. I kept telling the story, holding on to the "What ifs." "What if she stabbed me when she came into the kitchen and I was on the couch?" "What if she stole all my equipment in the home office?" I mean, I could have gone down the rabbit hole with all of these hypothetical situations.

The thing is, it takes time and personal work to move from victim land to the next phase in the journey. Even today when bad things happen, I start off in victim land and give myself time to be in that space, but I promise myself to swiftly move on because I know that I don't belong in victim land forever.

## What to Do in the Meantime

As I write this chapter, I'm going through a very difficult time in my life. I want to share something personal that I believe is a great example of how you can move from victim land into neutral land, while waiting for your road trip to victor land.

To make a long story short, my husband and I have been married for 4 years, and we've been trying to have a baby for 2 of those years. It's been a very long and painful journey. When you get to the point in life where you have the career, the house, the stable relationship and all that adult stuff people aspire to get, people often say things like, "When are you having a baby?" "Don't wait too long to have kids!" "Do you want kids?"

Yes, we do, but it's just been harder for us to get pregnant. A few weeks ago, I found out I was pregnant. We were so excited, we told our close friends and family members, picked a name, downloaded every pregnancy app we could find, and started making small actions towards this new life

we've both been waiting for.

Then during our first ultrasound, the day after Mother's Day and the day before my husband's birthday, the doctor told us the pregnancy isn't viable and told me to prepare for a miscarriage. I was devastated. This past week I've been in victim land. I've asked those questions, "Why me?" "Why does it always have to be something?" "When will I finally get my little baby?" I even took myself on a shame paved guilt trip and wondered if I was struggling to have a baby because of the abortion I had years ago when I got pregnant during a pretty rough time in my life.

I'm not going to lie to you; it's been a tough week full of tears, lying in bed with the curtains drawn, being anti-social, taking a social media break, and leaving text messages on read... I'm not feeling it this week.

## Feel All Those Emotions

I did make time for self-care though. I dragged myself out of the house to see my therapist, go to the gym, attend my acupuncture session (I literally just learned about acupuncture, Google it if you've never heard of it, it's very relaxing and healing!), write this book, and listen to uplifting music. I even chatted with my manager to let her know I'd need extra support over the next few weeks, possibly months.

I also let myself feel all the emotions that came up: anger, hurt, pain, guilt, all that. When we deny our emotions and bottle them up, that's when we get ourselves in trouble and explode in the future. Find a space to just let go, ugly cry and journal about all your feelings to get that stuff out of your body. We need to release it in order to heal.

By the end of the week, I could see the light at the end of the tunnel and although I have a long journey ahead of me, I know I will overcome. I know I'll share my story with other women when I heal completely, and I know it'll all be okay. I'm slowly walking myself into victor-land, but I'm neutral right now, and that's okay. For me, being neutral is letting go of the victim badge, taking care of myself and healing, but promising myself to make the trip to victor land sooner than later.

## Flourishing in Victor Land

I love this quote- "If you can look up, you can get up." Don't mope around with a "woe is me" complex for too long. I mean, you can give yourself a few days or a week, but we got to let that go. It doesn't do you or anyone else any good.

| I AM A VICTOR | I AM A VICTIM |
|---|---|
| *These situations don't define me. They are necessary for my journey toward growth.* | *My boss doesn't like me. They don't appreciate anything I do.* |
| *I've done my best. Things may not be great right now but I can choose my own future.* | *Why did God do this to me?* |
| *I am responsible for everything in my life.* | *If I put more into the relationship, maybe they would have stayed.* |
| *I can't change what happened but what can I do to change from this day forward?* | *I have no choice, this isn't my fault.* |
| *I accept what happened as part of life and choose to overcome this.* | *Why does everything bad always happen to me?* |

The moment I started feeling bad for myself and making excuses for why I didn't achieve certain goals, I began to adopt a victim mentality instead of a victor mentality. What's the difference? I'm so glad you asked.

If someone has a victim mentality, they recognize themselves as a victim of the negative actions of others or life, and tend to blame everyone else for their predicament.

However, once you adopt a victor mentality, you're communicating to yourself and the universe that you are going to be okay!

It's important to give ourselves time to tell our story, feel all those feelings and process the events that happened to us, but in order to be a victor, we must move on. You're safe now. You made it. You survived it.

So what will you do with all that energy ? Will you put it toward something positive or will you continue to parade around telling that victim story?

# Chapter 5
# Just Stir & Add Water

**When I was a sophomore in college, one of my friends invited me to a sorority campus party.**

She told me there would be boys, food, music, dancing, fun... and did I mention boys?

Well it didn't take much to convince me to find a cute outfit, do my hair and make-up, and head over to the Student Union Building (SUB), which wasn't too far from my dorm room.

I found a cute little black dress, slipped on my black heels and was ready to go.

We get to the SUB and it's packed. The party is already lit and I'm ready to have some fun. Being the greedy college student I was, I bee-lined straight to the food because if you know anything about college students, they're usually broke and hungry- or at least I was!

As I'm scarfing down my appetizer, I'm already thinking about the songs I want the DJ to play. Now I don't know about you, but my rhythm and dance moves are a little suspect- sometimes I'm good, other times, you'd be like, "What is you doing, girl?"

With this in mind, there are about 4 songs that make me get up and dance at any party or wedding. Can you guess what songs?

Any and all line dancing songs. The Electric Slide, the Cupid Shuffle, the Cha Cha Slide, and the Wobble. For people like me, these songs are usually safe because they literally tell you exactly what to do, you know?

As soon as I've moved on to my main course, guess what happens? My song comes on... The Cupid Shuffle. Before anybody even gets up to start dancing, I dart up to the dance floor and start doing my thing and other people start to join me. The dance floor quickly fills up quickly as other students watch us get into it.

*"Down, down, do your dance, do your dance. Down, down, do your dance, do your dance...To the right, to the right, to the right, to the right, to the left, to the left, to the left, to the left. Now kick, now kick, now kick, now kick, now walk it by yourself, now walk it by yourself..."*

## "And then things get really weird."

So we're all up there dancing and everything is cool... and then things get really weird.

I'm in the front row with everyone behind me. I go to do the next step in the song for "walk it by yourself" and I turn, now facing the crowd... and they're looking at me.

I'm so embarrassed and I'm low-key confused because this is my song. I know all the dance steps, and in order for me to be the only person facing the group behind me, that means something went wrong.

I slide off the dance floor trying not to be seen, and notice my home boy, Jared, is DJing, so I go over to him and ask, "Jared, did you see that? Am I doing something wrong?"

Jared is cracking up as he looks at me and yells over the music with a huge smile, "Nah, *they're* doing it wrong, they forgot the extra step. I noticed that too."

We both laughed and I went back on the dance floor to do MY dance, and confidently went against what the crowd was doing.

Like any other line dancing song, there are different styles, and the people that were on the dance floor that day did something different while I stuck with what I knew.

## How would you feel?

Imagine if you were me on the dance floor. How would you feel? Tons of people sitting at their tables with their eyes glued to a jam-packed dance floor- and I guess I should add- I was one of the few Black girls at the event.

Isn't it wild that we can be on the right track, doing what we're supposed to do... but if no one else around us is taking the right step- we feel out of place, like we're wrong?

## "It's ok to be alone. Being alone doesn't mean you're lonely."

This whole Cupid Shuffle experience taught me so much. As someone that used to hate being alone, and was

*Throwback to college days*

*Told you I stayed hungry LOL*

uncomfortable when I had to stand for what I believed in, even when no one else was rocking with me, this experience taught me that it's okay to be alone. Being alone doesn't mean you're lonely, and it doesn't mean you're wrong.

Sometimes the best thing you can do for yourself is to look around at everybody else and do the total opposite. It reminds me of when I was in high school- there were more than 5 girls that got pregnant together in my class, people were selling drugs, some people were into fighting and feeding off drama, there was a lot going on and not many people were doing what I was doing.

I wasn't an angel, but I was applying for scholarships, going to college visits, meeting with my guidance counselor so he could review my essays, and trying to prepare for my future.

## So why do you need to stir and add water?

This chapter is all about stirring and adding water, which represents the fact that you'll be shaking things up a bit in both your life and the lives of others as you make lemonade.

You'll need some valuable nuggets of wisdom in order to successfully make lemonade and dilute the sour taste of the lemons.

In this chapter, I'm going to share a few tips and mindset shifts with you that will allow you to walk with confidence, tap into your inner power, and feel whole- even when you're walking alone.

## Tip #1- Make Time to Be By Yourself

When I was in high school, I used to hate myself. I didn't feel pretty. I didn't like my body because I was super skinny, and "didn't have a shape", as many people would say. I was a late bloomer in every sense of the word. I had trouble seeing my worth because I was still impacted by the verbal and physical abuse I had gone through.

I used to always surround myself with a lot of noise and distractions in my life. I'd stay on the phone with friends for 5 hours so I wouldn't have to be by myself. I'd watch TV until I fell asleep. I'd stay on social media, refreshing my page to see if I got any new comments. I even kept toxic people around just so I wouldn't have to be alone. I kept myself occupied so I'd rarely have to sit by myself and be alone with my thoughts. My thoughts scared me because they were often really bad, hurtful, and depressing.

Years later, I learned that it's so important for us to embrace solitude and make time to be alone. I actually learned this when I went on that missions trip the day Daddy died. On that trip, we were encouraged to sit out in nature and journal, wake up in the morning and pray, and sit by ourselves in silence and meditate. At first it was awkward, but I began to realize that something magical can happen when we are by ourselves.

## Reasons Why It's Important to Embrace Solitude

**You get to meet yourself-** In the same way you meet other people, date them, or build relationships with them, we need to do the same for ourselves. Take time to find out what you like or dislike, what you need to heal, and what you want to accomplish in this world. This is the true glow up. I have so many friends that never took time for themselves and ended up getting married, having kids, and realizing later down the line that they never wanted that life for themselves in the first place. They looked lit and glow'd up on the outside, but were miserable on the inside. They didn't take time to be alone to figure out where they wanted the GPS of life to go, and got hijacked by other people who had different destinations in mind. Take time to be with yourself and get to know who you really are, especially before you partner up with someone and build a life.

**You get to reprogram your mind-** if you grew up around a lot of negativity and have bad thoughts about yourself, it's important to cancel out the negative with positive affirmations and self-love. The thing about affirmations is that it's important to say them out loud with confidence, even when you don't

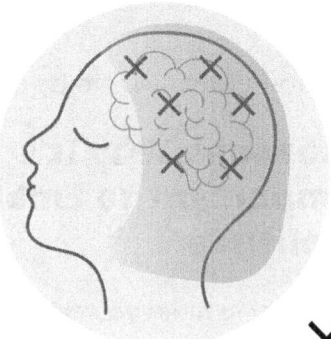
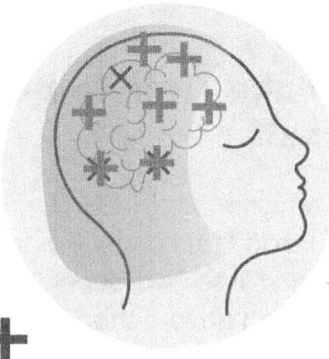
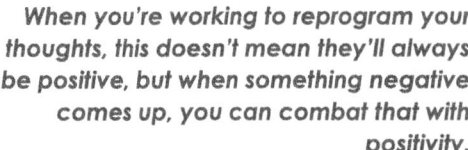

*When you're working to reprogram your thoughts, this doesn't mean they'll always be positive, but when something negative comes up, you can combat that with positivity.*

*If I make a mistake and there's a thought in my head that says, "You're so stupid." I'd say in mind to myself, "It's okay, you just made a mistake, you're still smart and valuable." Repeat this process ANY time a negative thought surfaces.*

## "If someone you love overheard your internal dialogue, what would they think? How you talk to yourself and how you talk about yourself is impacting the way you show up in life. Put some respect on your name."

believe them. It's like you're literally canceling out all the negatives with positives, so while it's going to take a lot of work- it's worth it. Another thing to keep in mind is that this is not an overnight process; you are doing the personal work necessary today, so you can live the life you want to live in the future.

**You become self-sufficient-** I got my first real taste of independence when I was in college. I had my own car, my own place, and I was paying my own bills. In addition to having my own, I was also working on being comfortable and confident with my independent thoughts. Spending time alone allowed me to gain a sense of self that no one else could take away. I'd come up with creative ideas like writing this book, starting my blog, starting a business- all things that I'd never have time to focus on if I didn't carve out time for myself. I'd go to the movies by myself, I'd go shopping alone and I felt that I had everything within me to make me feel good and whole. I'd even find myself in situations where I had an opinion that didn't align with the people I was with... and I felt okay with that. I felt like I was my own best friend. When I decided to make new friends or get into a relationship, it wasn't out of fear, the need to be with someone, or desperation. I chose them because I felt like they were good for me. I learned that I didn't need anyone else for internal happiness- and you don't either.

## Your Affirmation Bank

Affirmations are positive statements that can help you challenge and overcome self-defeating or negative thoughts. I'd encourage you to read your affirmations with confidence as you look yourself in the eyes in a mirror, although you can also say them as you're walking about or going about your day.

When you repeat your affirmations often, and believe in them and their power, you can truly start to make positive changes. An important thing to remember is to focus on the positive. If you're struggling with a negative thought pattern that keeps telling you, "You are an idiot," you don't want your affirmation to be, "I'm not an idiot." This is sort of like an empty statement because you're not canceling out "idiot" with something positive, right? You might instead say, "I am brilliant". Even if you don't feel brilliant, say it anyway!

I know sometimes it sounds crazy or unrealistic for some, but affirmations are like building the positivity muscles in your mind. You can't go to the gym once a month and expect to see lasting results. You must commit to the long haul and practice your affirmations at least 3 times a week, if not every day, and wait until you get results. **Here are some of my favorite personal affirmations:**

- ☐ **I am loved**
- ☐ **I am beautiful**
- ☐ **I'm smart**
- ☐ **I have the power to heal myself**
- ☐ **I am confident**
- ☐ **I belong here**
- ☐ **Everything I need is within me**
- ☐ **I've got this**

*Think about how you want to feel and what negative thoughts you plan to replace, and write your affirmations down below.*

## Tip #2- Make it a Priority to Learn and Grow

I had one of the strangest but most enlightening epiphanies at my job a few years ago. You know those disposal toilet seat covers that typically hang out in most public bathrooms in the big dispenser on the wall?

Well as a kid, my mom taught my sister and I the art of squatting so we never really used those annoying seat covers.

It wasn't until I was in high school that I started using the seat covers, and honestly... I never really liked them! It was more of a hassle for me, but it got to the point where I was tired of squatting. My thighs would burn (yea, I probably needed to work out more), my balance was off and sometimes the back of my leg would touch the toilet. YUCK!

At this point in life, I've been using toilet seat covers for more than 10 years. What I dislike most about the paper covers is the fact that they don't seem to stay where they're supposed to stay- on the toilet seat!

One time I placed the toilet seat cover neatly on the toilet, and as soon as I was about to use it... the automatic flush disrupted my whole set up and flushed the dang thing down the toilet.

Other times, if the AC was on high, the cover would almost fly away.

Earlier this year, my aunt shared a Facebook post that blew my mind! It was edifying but also left me feeling silly. Here's the post that had me dumbfounded. The caption read:

### "Tell me the truth, who knew this was the correct way to use a toilet seat cover?!? #mindblown"

All these darn years I was putting the toilet seat cover on the wrong way! I was placing the flap on the inside of the toilet which often resulted in the seat cover flushing down the toilet prematurely.

For more than 10 years, I misused this "resource" and never tried to find a new way to make it work for me, seek out alternatives or spark up a conversation with someone who

may have had a similar experience. I became complacent. I figured "This is just the way it is, I guess I have to deal with it."

Now clearly, this isn't that big of a deal but sometimes we have the same thought process for areas of our lives that DO matter. Our relationships, academics, sports, our purpose, misfortunes, finances, and the list goes on and on.

We can't seem to pass the test and accept the self-imposed narrative, "I guess I'll never get an A" or "I guess I wasn't meant to go to that school." Instead of being proactive, we become reactive.

We keep losing the game and can't seem to get it right, but instead of talking to the coach, creating a game plan or practicing until we get it right, we accept the narrative, "I'll do better next time", "I'm going to keep trying (the same thing that hasn't worked) until it works" or "Once I get in shape, I'll do XYZ"... but we don't follow through.

I'm sure you've heard that saying, "Insanity is doing the same thing over and over, expecting different results." This toilet seat cover situation convicted me in a way. The thing is, we must be committed to learning and growing if we want to become our best selves. Change can't be avoided, so we might as well go with it.

## How to Make Learning and Growing a Priority

**1. Ask questions and do your research**
We live in a world full of fake news and trolls, and sometimes it's really hard to determine where and what the truth is. Always question everything and do your own research, even when it's unpopular. Don't just go with the crowd. Don't just read the headline on social media or believe the news; do your own research and form your own opinion based on what you find. When I was in college, one of my mentors told me about a business opportunity where I could make some money. I was in a room full of adults, my mentor, her friends and the people who claimed they made a lot of money from this business.

Being the person I am, I raised my hand during the question-and-answer session and asked the person speaking if I could see proof that he made the money he claimed he made. My mentor went off! She scolded me in front of the group, and I felt so embarrassed and small. I didn't realize it in the moment, but I did the right thing. I didn't just believe the guy who said he made money because I didn't see any proof. I wanted to make sure that before I signed up for this business that would cost me money, it'd be

worth my time and investment. Just as a side note, many of the people that were in that room that day are no longer in that business. Imagine that...

**2. Know that it's ok when you don't know the answer -** There's nothing worse than talking to someone that's BSing you because they don't have the courage to say, "I don't know." One of my personal affirmations that keeps me humble and confident is, "I have something to learn and something to teach." I usually say this before I go into meetings or gatherings with people who don't look like me, and when my negative self-talk tries to creep in and tell me I don't belong. You also have something to learn and something to teach. When you don't know something, embrace it and seek out the answer. The smartest people are usually the ones that ask the most questions, and oftentimes when you ask a "silly question", there are others in the room wondering the same thing.

**3. Be open to constructive feedback-** I get a lot of compliments these days on my public speaking skills. To me, it's bizarre because when I first started out, I was the worst public speaker ever! I started speaking in church when I was about 14 years old. My parents would volunteer (more like voluntold) me to read the scripture, share my thoughts on a sermon, and do things in front of the congregation. At first, I'd be super nervous. My voice would shake and I felt like I was about to cry from stage fright and I'd talk fast with hopes of jetting off the stage as soon as I was finished. However, the more I did it, the more comfortable I became.

Today, I travel around the country to speak at middle schools, high schools, and colleges as a motivational speaker. I've been on this motivational speaking journey for about 7 years now. The reason I've gotten so good at it, is because I've practiced. More importantly, my mentors have watched me speak. When I first started out, they'd pull me to the side after I got off stage and run down a list of things I did well and another list of what I could improve upon.

I ALWAYS wrote down the areas for improvement and studied them so I could become better. Not only did I write them down and ask questions, I tweaked my speech, added their feedback, and had them judge me again until I improved. There were other speakers I started out with that couldn't take the feedback; it was a huge hit to their ego and they decided to stick with the way they've been doing things. When we refuse to change, we can't grow and get better.

**4. Promise yourself to become a life-longer learner -** Being a life-long learner doesn't mean you'll be sitting in a classroom for the rest of your life (even though that wouldn't be a bad idea). What it means is that you are open to learning at every stage of your journey. Try new things, be open-minded, read, listen to podcasts, and find ways to expand your horizons. I'm a big nerd and love learning, and I've become okay with that the older I get. I realize this isn't a dating book, but I have to say, being smart and knowing a little about a lot makes you more attractive and interesting to others too.

Being a life-long learner also means getting outside of your comfort zone and leaving the place where you grew up. Even though I grew up poor, I was exposed to different lifestyles, and my parents always made sure I could travel to different neighborhoods and cities in the U.S. to see how people lived, what they ate, and what their culture was like. Please, whatever you do, travel as much as you can. When you see more of the world, you'll want more for yourself. You'll see people just like you- that come from where you come from- out here making it and living their best lives.

## Tip #3 Determine What a Confident You Looks Like

Traveling on this journey through womanhood, has been a roller coaster, to say the least, especially when it comes to defining "me" and my confidence. Over the past few years, one of my goals has remained the same: gain more confidence. There have been several occasions when I've Googled things like "How to get more confidence", "Qualities of a strong Black woman", "What does it mean to be confident?", the list could go on.

## Confidence is Subjective

I believe that confidence is subjective and also situational. It's subjective because YOU define what it means to be a confident you. I've found that for me, a "confident Terri" means that: I'm comfortable in my skin, regardless of who's in my presence, I walk with my head up and think positive thoughts while doing so, I voice my opinion, I treat myself with respect and demand that others do the same, and I refrain from comparing myself to others.

These are just a few of the rules that contribute to my confidence. I'll admit, sometimes I break the "confidence rules", and find myself feeling self-conscious or insecure. But because I've made my own rules, I

know what thoughts lead me back to feeling and being more confident. Write your name in the blank space on the right and jot down the qualities of a confident you.

## Confidence is Situational

Today, if you were to put me in front of a group of teenage girls and you told me to speak with them about overcoming adversity, I'd be able to effortlessly and fearlessly put something together on the spot. I'd be confident and at ease. However, if you were to ask me to give a presentation on global warming to the same group of girls, I'd probably be nervous and unsure of myself.

I've spent the past few years creating, revising and presenting workshops on overcoming adversity, which contributes to my confidence in that area. On the other hand, I'm not well versed on the topic of global warming, and unfortunately, I don't have a passion to speak to young girls about it (though it'd be wise to know about this subject!).

We usually have more confidence in our abilities when we're comfortable and familiar in a given situation, thus making confidence situational.

**What does a confident _____ look like?**

**What situations or environments are you naturally confident in?**

## How You Can Gain More Confidence

If you're like me and you want to gain more confidence, the first step is to figure out what you want to gain confidence in. "Gaining confidence" is a pretty vague goal that'll be difficult to reach, considering that you can't really measure it. Do you want to gain confidence in your appearance? Your public speaking? Your cooking? Your writing? Your ability to handle conflict?

Figure out what areas you want to gain confidence in, and set small goals that'll help you reach your desired outcomes. For instance, when I first started grad school, I was a hot mess! I say that because I had just

gotten out of a stressful relationship, I was starting a new job, living in a new area and on top of that, going to a new school. But not just a new school, GRAD SCHOOL! (I'm so dramatic, right?!) I was so nervous and unsure of myself. I wasn't confident in my academic or intellectual abilities, which caused me to shy away from speaking up in class. I didn't think I had anything significant to offer, and I also thought my classmates were way smarter than me.

Over the course of the semester, my mentor and I came up with a plan to help me gain more confidence when speaking up in class. One of my goals was to ask at least 3 questions per class. Sometimes, I'd even prepare questions before attending class to help with my nerves, and my mentor would check in with me bi-weekly to see how I was doing. Long story short, by the end of the semester, I turned into "that girl." That girl that always asks a million and one questions in class. But guess what? I started speaking up in class naturally and confidently. I also stopped caring about what others thought of me and my questions.

# THE CONFIDENCE GAME PLAN

**1.** Write down a few areas you want to become more confident in. Underneath, jot down a few baby steps that will help you reach your confidence goal. Use my examples as a reference.

**2.** Think about your future self and who you're becoming, and journal about who that person is. What does your confidence level look like? How do you walk into a room? What affirmations do you repeat to yourself?

## What You Need To Know About Body Image and Confidence

From tummy teas to waist trainers, Kim Kardashian's recent ad for an appetite suppressant lollipop, and thousands of social media posts dedicated to comparing bodies with rated numbers, social media impacts our perception of body goals, body image, and confidence, whether we want to admit it or not.

## Are Body Goals Realistic?

I've had several chats with my girlfriends recently, and many of us fall victim to the unrealistic "body goals" presented on social media. You're either not thick enough, skinny enough, or curvy enough, and sometimes it makes you question yourself after scrolling down your timeline.

Recently, a friend who was very thin growing up opened up to me and shared that she's embarrassed to post pictures of her body on social media because she doesn't want people to think she let herself go since she's gained some weight. She only posts pictures from the chest up.

Ugh! How did we get here?

Social media in particular has become a breeding ground for self-consciousness, based on very unrealistic and often flat out unrealistic expectations of how women (and men) should look and exist in their bodies. We focus so much on the physical glow up, when the most important glow up is the growth and level up that happens internally.

**So how do we take our power back? How do we maintain a groundedness in these vessels we live in without constantly reevaluating and judging ourselves against the "body goals" of social media?**

**1. Change the narrative:** The ways that we talk to ourselves matters. While scrolling through social media, be conscious of how you are practicing self-talk. You don't have to make a comparative statement every time you see a body you find fabulous. "Wow she looks great!" does not have to be followed up with, "I wish I looked like her."

**2. Follow accounts that affirm your glory:** Take time to take a peek at the hashtags #BodyPositivity #BoPo #BodyLove and #EffYourBeautyStandards to open yourself to a whole new world of self love! You could also follow people who look like you and have similar body types. This can be a great source of fashion inspiration and serve as a reminder to love yourself no matter what.

**3. Time shift:** Use 15-20 minutes of the time you might usually spend scrolling social media to show your body some love! Dry brushing (Google it), self massages, hot showers, bubble baths, or even a gentle self-hug are all things you can intentionally and actively do to take a stand against society's imposed expectations.

**4. Follow Lizzo and listen to her music:** Lizzo is an American singer, rapper, performer, and body positivity advocate. Just follow her work and you'll see why I recommended it.

**5. Rummage through The Body Is Not An Apology blog:** This blog is radically changing the ways we think about our bodies. I truly suggest that you explore its posts, resources and inspiration for a boost of confidence and understanding around your relationship with your body.

**6. Find India Arie's song, Private Party and listen to the song as you read the lyrics:** This was one of the most pivotal songs on my journey to self-love and self-acceptance. In the song, India Arie walks you through her journey of loving herself, and offers some good advice that we can use to love ourselves and our bodies as we grow and evolve. Self-love is an inside job, and it's something we'll be working at for the rest of our lives.

**7. Take time to reflect on your own internal understandings of beauty and where they may have come from:** Was your mom always commenting on her arms, and now you're prone to take a second glance at your own arms in the mirror? Were the girls at your school often immaturely squeamish about body hair and you've carried that into your adulthood? Reflect on your own body story, and make the necessary changes to ensure you're holding enough space to love yourself unconditionally.

**Repeat after me: "My body is the temple I inhabit, manage, love and indulge in. I make all decisions in how it exists."**

## You are Body Goals and Don't You Forget It

There are a few very important things I need you to know. Beauty is a business, an industry! Companies are profiting off of our insecurities every day. Don't let them! You have every right to feel beautiful exactly as you are. No rules, standards or expectations have to change that.

Lastly, please know in the climate we live in of #bodygoals, loving yourself is a revolution! Go be bold in self-love, self-care and the incredible power you have to be beautiful just as you are.

Imma need us to stop saying everyone else is body goals- especially when we don't have their medical file or know their daily struggles. What if YOU are body goals?

## You Don't Need a Big Butt to Be Attractive or Confident

You don't need a big butt, big breasts, or a snatched waist to be sexy or attractive. Sexiness, confidence, and high self esteem comes from within. I used to be so insecure because of my petite frame. Remember how I told you people called me sticks, said I was shaped like a boy, and said I had chicken legs etc...?

Over the years I've learned to love my body by using the tips I shared with you. Today, I work out regularly, eat healthy, and build the body I want in the gym. But even if you don't do any of that, you're still worthy. My boobs, they're what I call "Barely B's" (B cups), one is bigger than the other, I have stretch marks, hyperpigmentation, and a bunch of other flaws that many don't highlight on social media.

Who cares though? Like really... A bad body and big butt doesn't keep a man or woman. A bad body and big butt doesn't make you happy. Clarity, wholeness, and purpose is what I'm shooting for. This earthly body serves me well by allowing me to drive my mission and make an impact. When we die, this body will be futile. Our spirit though that's the real us.

You know what I've noticed? The world treats us the way we demand to be treated. When I began to love myself, and saw the value in my true essence and the internal glow up along with my outward appearance, people began to treat me with more respect, and I realized that they were taking cues from me. If they saw that I respected myself by what I allowed and how I carried myself, they respected me too. We have so much power, but this whole self-love journey begins on the inside.

**When it comes to body image, we have to remember not to project our feelings and opinions onto others. It's not right or wise to assume that we know how someone else feels about themselves, based on how we perceive them to be. Ladies, we should never speak down on another woman, let alone because of her weight. Society already does a damn good job of this!**

## Reminders for us all

**1. Changing your body for your partner is never a good idea -** If someone is pressuring you to get enhancements, they're saying you're not good enough the way you are. That's unacceptable and just not true! Leave them immediately.

**2. A big butt and snatched waist won't keep a man (or woman) -** We can literally go to social media for evidence here. Beautiful women we see or follow have the "perfect" hourglass shape, but this doesn't ensure their partner is faithful or stays with them for life.

**3. Self-love comes from within -** Many of the people we see focusing on their outward appearance are overcompensating for the lack of love within. Focus on being okay inside because if you don't love yourself inside, you'll run into a vicious cycle where you're constantly trying to change things on the outside in search of internal peace and validation.

**4. A healthy body is the best body -** You can research all the women and girls who've lost limbs, suffered from health disorders or even died trying to get a new body. A healthy you is truly the best you.

**5. When you love yourself unconditionally, those around you won't have any choice but to follow your lead -** You teach the world how to treat you by what you allow. When I began to love myself and my shape, others followed suit because if someone is so confident and in love with themselves, it's hard to feel any

different. You begin to see that person the way they see themselves and the way they demand to be treated.

## The Moment You've Been Waiting For

Can you believe the book is almost over? That was fast, right? We've come a long way.

I started off by telling you a little bit about my story and why you should even read this book. Then we dove right into the Big Pitcher, and if you've been following along, you've noticed that there were a lot of people supporting me along my journey. Even though I didn't have the best or most traditional family structure, my support came from good people that believed in me and I allowed them to support me because I knew I couldn't do it on my own.

Next, we moved on to the Main Squeeze. Just like squeezing a stress ball can relieve stress and provide therapeutic benefits, squeezing your lemons can do the same. Sometimes you can get lemon juice in your eyes or the eyes of those around you, which makes the process painful and risky at times. That's why we need a solid pitcher. Squeezing my lemons was tough because it was uncomfortable, but it forced me to grow and face my obstacles head on which was so necessary, and I'd do it all over again if I had to.

The third chapter, the Sugar F.A.C.E, was eye-opening for me. I was confused that I could do all the things, check off all the boxes, and have what looked like an amazing life on the outside... but still be haunted by the unresolved issues from my childhood and the trauma I'd experienced. In this chapter, we talked about forgiving yourself, addressing conflict constructively, choosing your own adventure from the end to the beginning, and embracing a victor-hood mentality.

Just Stir and Add Water is where the real glow up happens or the internal growth that allows you to exude light, love and healing for others. We talked about how self-love is an inside job and how important solitude is, among other things.

Now we're about to make our way into the last chapter. We're close to the end, but there's still more I need to share with you, so buckle up and let's get ready to make some lemonade, my friend!

# Chapter 6
# Make Lemonade and Share it

**Throughout this book I've shared with you some of the most life-changing moments from my journey. Some of them included accomplishments while others highlighted the sour lemons I thought would surely take me out.**

## There's Nothing Special About Me

I didn't grow up and glow up on my own.

I had different pitchers to support me along the way. I'm not special and I'm no different than you. I just didn't give up and did the work.

I leaned on my pitchers for support.

I squeezed my lemons and faced my problems head on.

I added a little bit of sugar to develop myself along the way.

I stirred and added water to dilute the sour taste of the lemons.

Last but certainly not least, I made lemonade and shared it with the world. This book is a glass of my best lemonade, just for you!

I hope that my story shows you that you are not defined by where you come from, what you come from, what happened to you, or how you got here. You truly have the power to make your wildest dreams come true. If I can do it, you can too!

## "I low key thought I'd get a book deal, get signed, or get discovered at the conference."

Ever since I was a teenager, I knew I wanted to write a book. I never thought I was a good writer but I knew I had a bunch of stories to tell. Plus, I've been journaling since I was in elementary school. Writing was my therapy before actually going to therapy.

When I was 18 years old, I wrote my first book and I was so excited to share my work with the world. I had done some research online and found this Christian Writer's conference where authors could go to learn more about how to write a book, and get a chance to share their work with editors from different publishing houses. This means I'd be in front of the very people who could help me publish my first book and get my message out to the world!

I wanted in, but there was only one problem- I was a broke college student and didn't have the money. After thinking about this conference long and hard, I finally told my grandmother (Mommom) about the conference and asked her if I could "borrow" the hundreds of dollars I'd need for registration and lodging.

I didn't know how I was going to pay her back, but I was determined to make it to this conference and figure out how to get Mommom's money back.

Mommom is so dope! She's always helping other people and even when she doesn't have it, she makes a way out of no way. She pulled me aside one day, took a wad of cash out of her bra and said, "Baby, this is all I have but I want you to go to that conference because I believe in you."

## The Sandy Cove Christian Writers Conference

I packed up my jeep and drove a little over an hour to North East, Maryland to attend my first big girl conference by myself. I was rooming with two older black women I met in the roommate search group the conference host put together.

I was nervous, but also extremely happy because I was proud of my work and low-key thought I'd get a book deal, get signed, or get discovered at the conference.

I thought I'd finally be able to pay Mommom back and inspire other people with my story.

# Sometimes a Setback is a Setup for a Comeback

To make a long story short, the conference was lit and I made a lot of great connections. I met with an editor and basically... my book was trash with a capital T. Yes, my feelings were hurt in the moment as I watched the editor critique my work, and challenge the ideas, concepts, and perspectives I shared. But look, let me just tell you- the new me is so freaking happy I never published that book.

I've grown so much since that time that I'd be embarrassed if that book was out with my name on it. I still have the manuscript and the paper the woman edited and... yes, my book was trash. I just didn't realize it back then. Guess what the title was by the way? "EXPOSED." Yeah, it was terrible. I was pretty discouraged and didn't try to write another book until years later. Sometimes a setback is a setup for a comeback.

Out of all the connections I made and all the experiences I had at that conference, one stuck with me and made me change my life. Looking back, I think I was meant to go to that conference for this one conversation.

## One of the Best Pieces of Advice I've Ever Gotten

Here's what happened. I'm at the conference and mind you, I'm one of the youngest people there, so I pretty much stand out in every room and dining hall we attend.

During one of the breaks one day, I'm chatting with this radio host named Deborah Johnson and she's really intrigued by my story. Mrs. Deborah is asking me all kinds of questions and we're having a really good conversation. Then she stares at me and asks intently, "So Terri, how did you make it? How did you overcome all you've experienced?"

Without even thinking about the question I blurted out, "God is good! I did a lot of praying." Mrs. Deborah sort of blankly stared at me, then dropped one the best pieces of advice I've ever received.

She said, "That's amazing and I don't doubt you did a lot of praying and I agree, God is good. The thing is, when you go share your story, write your books and give speeches, people are going to want action steps. Like, how can they too overcome? What practical tips or words of wisdom can you share with them? Prayer is great, but really think about what else you did; figure out how you overcame so you can truly help others."

## Be Who You Needed When You Were Younger

Mrs. Deborah left me speechless. I never looked at my story or life experiences in that way. I was so busy trying to survive, that I didn't even think about how to help others thrive and overcome the same things I'd experienced. For instance, I was super preachy in my first book, and the editor told me that I could turn people off from finishing the book based on the language I was using.

After this conference, I began to look at my life differently. Anytime something unfortunate happened, I'd give myself time and space to cry and be angry or feel whatever emotions I felt, but then I started journaling about how I actually got over break ups, how I overcame my fear of public speaking, how I overcame low self-esteem, etc. I started documenting the how behind my story so I could write books like this and help other people overcome their obstacles. I figured if I was going through this tough situation, I might as well pay it forward and give someone else the cheat code on how I made it so they can too.

Even though you may not be who you're going to become, you can still help others. There are kids in your community, students at your school, coworkers at your job, maybe even your cousins or siblings that look up to you, so if you become who you needed when you were younger and remember how you overcame what you've experienced, you can truly make lemonade and share it.

Writing this book is my way of walking through all the steps we talked about then sharing my lemonade with you. I'm pouring you a glass of lemonade from my experience. But I'm not the end all, be all. There are people in the world that won't connect with my story or resonate with me or my message and that's where you come in. You have something unique to offer this world, and it doesn't require you to shout your story and personal business from the rooftops.

You can pull that friend who's struggling with a toxic home life aside, and encourage them by sharing how you dealt with negativity in your own life. You can talk to that one family member who doesn't see her worth, tell her that she's beautiful, and give her advice and tools for boosting her self-esteem. You can share lemonade in your corner of the world and make an impact- that's just as important as any other motivational speaker or author.

## "When you live your truth, nobody can use your truth against you." - Charlamagne Tha God

I've always known I had a story to tell, but I didn't see myself as the hero. I longed for validation and saving. I literally used to dream about Oprah discovering me one day and changing my whole life. I thought the only way I'd make it out of poverty was to get "put on."

It wasn't until I was in college that I realized that no one was going to save me- it's all on me. I am my own hero. The only way my life will change is if I muster up the courage and strength to do something about it. I must go from being a victim complaining about what happened to me and who did what, and become the victor of my story. I must put myself on and you must do the same.

I used to be really shy and embarrassed of where I come from, but as I began to share my story with a few friends here and there, they were deeply inspired by what I've been through. This gave me boldness to share my story on a larger scale because I knew that I was onto something; I was impacting people.

Charlamagne Tha God said it best, "When you live your truth, nobody can use your truth against you." As I began to own my story and share details about living in a shelter, being molested, being broke, and dealing with depression, I felt strong! What could anyone say to me after I already told my truth? It is what it is, and the beautiful thing about the story is those dark places are just the beginning- my story gets better and yours can too!

The thing about sharing your story is starting small and sharing with positive people who will uplift you. As you get more comfortable, you can share it widely if you so choose.

Now that I've told you about a lot of the stuff I've been through, I want to share with you how I'm constantly becoming the hero of my story, over and over again. Take a look at some of my accomplishments on the next page. I achieved all of these things before the age of 30.

# My Accomplishments

When I was 21 years old, I was the commencement speaker at my college graduation. My parents couldn't make it but I had solid pitchers there to support me.

I started a podcast with a friend and literally Googled every step of the process because I had no idea what I was doing.

I started my own online business (using Google and YouTube as my teachers) and learned how to make thousands online by teaching people how to blog and build brands.

I organized an event for women of color at the tech company I work at in San Francisco. We had such a great turnout!

I graduated with my Masters of Arts in Conflict Analysis and Dispute Resolution from Salisbury University at the age of 23.

I became a motivational speaker!

When I was 27 years old I started making 6 figures from various streams of income which includes my day job, motivational speaking, and my online business.

I started a blog for women called, Mocha Girls Pit Stop, when I was in grad school.

## Keep Track of Your Accomplishments

When you look at the things I've accomplished over the course of the past few years, I hope you're encouraged by the fact that it all started somewhere. Every journey begins with one little step- not two, not three, not 100- just one. Back in the day, I remember when my three biggest accomplishments were preparing a Thanksgiving meal on my own, registering my siblings for school, and graduating from high school. We gotta put some respect on our small wins so we can get to the big wins.

After you take a look at my accomplishments, I want you to start adding pictures to your own accomplishments highlight reel on the following page. You can add pictures, write words, share memories, whatever you need to do to showcase the things you've done that make you feel good. Document them and revisit them often.

I have an accomplishments book to this day where I store all my wins, and trust me, it comes in handy when you're having a bad day and need some inspiration.

# My Accomplishments

# So, What's Next You Ask?

Ayee! You did it. You stuck with me until the end, but now what?

Well here's one thing, I hope this wasn't just another book to you. I really hope that you connected with at least one perspective or story because I'm gonna be real, I legit gave you some of my most life-changing cheat codes that you can use on your journey to better yourself and those around you. The thing is, everyone won't peep them and everyone won't take action.

But I hope that's not the case for you.

See, when I was a freshman in college, we had a motivational speaker come visit us right before the school year began. He gave a really funny speech, but one thing he said stood out and stuck with me all this time. The other students and I were seated in the auditorium, a group of us on one half and another group on the other.

The speaker's name was Carlos Ojeda Jr. and he said, "I want this half of the auditorium to stand up while the other side stays seated. In 4 years, only half of you will graduate." He went on to explain that based on statistics, only half of us would make it. Some would struggle financially and have to dropout, some might have babies and take a break, and other students might lose interest and fail out.

Carlos' words stuck with me, and I was determined to be one of the students that graduated in 4 years - and I was, despite all that I had experienced. The world is so small that when I was in graduate school, one of my college advisors connected me with Carlos and he became my mentor. I later started speaking for his company, CoolSpeak. Crazy right?

## But Here's the Moral of the Story...

You read the book, you have the tools, so how you gonna act? Are you going to go back to your usual life or are you going to shift your thinking and begin implementing these cheat codes in your own life?

For the trailblazers and the real ones that really want to rise above the obstacles, I have some next steps for you. It's been such a pleasure being on this journey with you. Thank you for being here. Thank you for motivating me to keep pushing. You make my journey worth every sad night that I cried myself to sleep.

# Your Next Steps

 If you connected with anything in this book, tell me! I'd love to know. Enter your email address at this link (**glowupbook.com**) and shoot me an email to share your thoughts.

 If you were inspired by anything in this book, share it with a friends, coworkers, teachers, mentors, or anyone that may benefit from the stories and resources. I'd be happy to speak at your school, event, or conference!

 Every Friday, my cohost and I release episodes on the H.E.R. Space Podcast. We're on iTunes, Spotify, SoundCloud, GooglePlay and most places podcasts are played. Come hang out with us!

 I teach people how to start podcasts and build their brands online, take a look at my next inspirational masterclass on **terrilomax.com**.

 Based on what we've discussed in this book, answer these 3 questions. What will you stop? What will you continue? and What will you change?

 Take a look at the list on the next page and get inspired to do great things!

# Most likely to succeed

### Terri Lomax
Overcame statistics about children with incarcerated parents. **She is a Podcaster, speaker, and businesswoman.**

### Carlos Ojeda Jr.
Overcame statistics about inner city latino youth and hearing impairment. **He is a dynamic speaker, author, CEO of a million-dollar company, CoolSpeak, and father of 3.**

### April Hernandez-Castillo
Saved herself from a violent intimate relationship. **She is an actress, author, and speaker and has been on Law & Order, Dexter and had a lead role in the movie, Freedom Writers.**

### Ernesto Mejia
Proud son of Mexican immigrants. diagnosed with Guillain-Barré Syndrome at 16 years old. **He is a world-class facilitator, author, Co-founder of a million-dollar company, CoolSpeak, and father of 3.**

### Tim Stafford
His biggest challenge was overcoming self-doubt. **His biggest accomplishment is performing at poetry festivals throughout Europe.**

### Rhett Burden
Craniosynostosis rendered him intellectually inept early on in life and has left a permanent scar down the middle of his head. **He is an author, speaker, and educator and was inducted into his alma mater's (UMES) Hall of Excellence.**

## Jasmine Green

Her biggest challenge was overcoming self. When she realized that she served as the ultimate block in her personal & business development, she began taking intentional steps to reinvent the stories she'd tell herself....about herself. **She is a successful business coach and entrepreneur who has helped her clients create massive impact by leveraging their unique gifts to serve others.**

## Zo Williams

Born as the last child of 6 to his 27-year-old mother, he was adopted at a young age along with his older brother. **He is an author, relationship expert, entrepreneur, and intellectual.**

_____ (You)

_____
_____
_____
_____
_____
_____
_____
_____
_____
_____
_____
_____
_____
_____

## Lisa Nichols

From a struggling single mom on public assistance to **a millionaire entrepreneur, author, and speaker**, her courage and determination has inspired millions worldwide and helped countless audiences breakthrough, to discover their own untapped talents and infinite potential.

Made in the USA
Middletown, DE
18 August 2020